A
Bridge
Over
Troubled Water

Renee' Drummond-Brown

AuthorHouse™
1663 Liberty Drive
Bloomington, IN 47403
www.authorhouse.com
Phone: 1 (800) 839-8640

Scripture quotations marked KJV are from the Holy Bible, King James Version (Authorized Version). First published in 1611. Quoted from the KJV Classic Reference Bible, Copyright © 1983 by The Zondervan Corporation.

Published by AuthorHouse 12/27/2018

ISBN: 978-1-5462-5598-7 (sc)
ISBN: 978-1-5462-5600-7 (hc)
ISBN: 978-1-5462-5599-4 (e)

Library of Congress Control Number: 2018909610

Print information available on the last page.

Any people depicted in stock imagery provided by Getty Images are models,
and such images are being used for illustrative purposes only.
Certain stock imagery © Getty Images.

This book is printed on acid-free paper.

authorHOUSE®

A Bridge Over Troubled Water

Introduction

Stepping out of fear and trusting faith is challenging. Faith of a mustard seed. Faith that one can do all things. Faith of believing on things hoped for and not seen. This faith has given me a vision, mission, purpose and goal to become a catalyst for the plight of African American people and write prose with such conviction that is sure to rouse the soul, touch the broken heart, and ultimately transform one's mind. There is a call on my life and responsibility, where I have been moved to step out of fear and act on faith to pick up the mantle of the great poets before me and get to gentler terms to bridge the conversation concerning African American people and their complexed history relating to slavery, Civil Rights and injustices in the 21st century. Like a bridge over troubled waters, I will lay me down and go beyond my call of duty to write the wrongs truthfully.

My collection of poems governing theme(s) will address the legal institution of human enslavement, primarily Afro-Americans, documented injustices which reflect periods in time relating to the *Civil Rights Movement* era, the twenty-first century and focus on the truth, the whole truth, and nothing but the truth. Because I am a black woman, born in the 60's, down South, during the Civil Rights Movement era, I connect with the Negro dialect associated with both Paul Laurence Dunbar and Dr. Maya Angelo's poetry. Their literary influence mystified my mind and made me want to investigate more about the plight of my people and share what I learn with the world.

After taking Rhetoric of the Civil Rights Movement class while at Geneva College and traveling on the "13th Annual Returning to the Roots of Civil Rights Bus Tour" and also Kenya, Africa, I developed a burning desire to make an impact on the world as it relates to a pattern of familiar discriminations on African Americans. My vision is *Renee's Poems with Wings are Words in Flight* becoming a household name globally while depositing historical facts in poetic fashion that are sure to develop and awaken the soul. My mission is to put prose into action metaphorically pointed, with images designed to have colorblind justice, hear the truth touch freedom and taste love in poetic fashion. The purpose is to bridge the gap of philosophies, without biases, that will enlighten and unify the human race through the genre of poetic accounts. My goal is to educate the human race, by bridging their knowledge and furthermore reminding the African American people that we cannot forget to remember our past and we cannot remember to forget our present and we should never forget that we were sold to the highest bidder.

A Bridge Over Troubled Water Contents

Introduction iii

Affirmation ix

Acknowledgements: xii

Renee's Quotes: xvii

Renee's Rhythm and Poetic Blues Category: 2

   A BRIDGE OVER TROUBLED WATER 3

   A Quiet Storm 5

   ABORT THE MISSION 7

   ACE. OF SPADE 9

   Against the Winds 13

   Ain't Got Nothin' But Pride 14

   ALL God's Childrens' Ain't Got "Heavy" Shoes! 16

   ANGRY BLACK WOMEN 18

   Baby 20

   Bad boyz' bad boyz' what cha gone do? 21

   BLACK CRIMES MATTER! 23

   BLACK PANTHER 25

   "Blacky" 28

   Border 29

   Brown's Truth 30

   Call Me Out My Name Again! 31

   Colored Gal; How Dare You? 32

Cut from A Different Cloth..34

Don't Burn Your Bridge!...36

Eye Spy A Lie...38

Fatigued 40

Fragile Handle with Care (CRACKED up)! 41

I Am Woman; Hear 'Me' Roar!...43

I Know Why The Caged Byrd Sangs 48

I'LL SAY IT LOUD! I'M BLACK AND I'M PROUD!! 52

'Ima Colored Girl 54

London Bridge Is Falling Down 56

Long Live the Queen ARETHA FRANKLIN 58

My Best Isn't Good Enough 60

Negronis' We Get You 61

Nowhere Ov'r the Rainbow..62

Phillis Wheatley 63

POETRY 66

Raccoon 67

Still I Write (The Answer to: Dr. Maya Angelou's "Still I Rise")....................68

Titanic 72

Wisdom Seeds 74

WOMAN..75

Xenophobic 76

Societal Issues Category: 77

400 Years 78

1961..83

A, B, C Easy as 1, 2, 3..84

A Child of God? 86

And A Child Shall Lead Them? 87

Another one bites the dust... and another one of "US" gone. 89

BLACK ON BLACK RACISM 91

Cycles 95

EENY MEENY MINY MOE 96

FATHER DEAREST 97

Half Blood..99

HOW DARE YOU! 100

Liberty an jUStice for Sum 102

PREDICAMENT 104

Same 'Ole Sad Song...105

Seasons in the Sun...106

The Chicken's Finally Came Home to Roost...108

THE DOOR OF NO RETURN 110

We Rode On The Bones Of A Slave...112

Love Category:..115

A Mother's Love Returned 116

Drowned in One's Own Blood 118

Little 'girlz..119

Peace Be Still 121

Stalker..124

Spiritual Category:...127

Give to the Poor..128

God, What Do You Want from Me?...129

Sisters Still Standing 131

THE PERFECT RUNWAY MODEL 133

The True Vine 134

THIS LAND IS RAVEN'S LAND 136

Civil Rights Category:..137

"4 Little Girls" 138

BLOODY SUNDAY!..140

BLOODY SUNDAY MARCHES ON TUESDAY! 141

Emmett Louis Till; Sleep My Child and Finally Get Some Rest 142

Eyes off the Prize?..144

Fit For a 'King' 147

MS. RUTHA MAE HARRIS 151

Rutha's Freedom Still Dreams! 153

Tide Can't Get These Stains Out! 156

Whistle Blowers 158

'X' Marks the Spot! 159

Slavery Category:...162

25 Lashes..163

America was Raised on 'MY' Breast..165

δοῦλος [Doulos] 169

Flesh of My Flesh! 170

He Beat Me 171

"him!" 172

Negro HAND Me Downs and BRASS feet JUST Like Mine...........173

Ocean Blue, What color are you? 176

Slave Gal; Miss Mary Mack Ain't got 'Nothin' On You!................178

SLAVERY Recipe 180

Still Waters Run Deep 182

Wade in the Water 184

WHO LET THE 'DAWGZ' OUT?...186

Sympathy Category: 190

A Caged Bird Sings...191

Aged to Perfection..193

BIRD CAGE 195

Boy...197

Golgotha..199

Jaws (dun ta dun ta dun ta dun) 200

let it snow. let it snow. let it snow...201

Root Canal 202

Specks' of Dust 206

THE cart before the horse 207

Trail of Tears 209

21st Century Category: 211

Bird's Eye View 212

Can't We All Just Get Along? Hell Naw! 213

GARAGE SALE- (EVERYTHANG MUST GO)!!! 215

IF, Innocent. Why Run? 218

Let's Make America Great Again 219

PLAN B in 'da house! 221

Sequestered 223

Sick and Tired of Y'our' Freedom? 224

Tainted 225

Tar Baby 226

The Central Park 5 228

The Choice is Up to You? 231

What's A Stud to Do? 235

You ain't 'gone believe this… GUESS WHAT I HEARD? 239

Indebtedness to: 240

Biography 241

Affirmation

A Psalm of David

"The Lord is my shepherd;
I shall not want.
He maketh me to lie down in green pastures:
he leadeth me beside the still waters.
He restoreth my soul:
he leadeth me in the paths of righteousness for his name's sake.
Yea,
though I walk through the valley of the shadow of death,
I will fear no evil:
For thou art with me;
thy rod and thy staff they comfort me.
Thou preparest a table before me in the presence of mine enemies:
thou anointest my head with oil;
my cup runneth over.
Surely goodness and mercy shall follow me all the days of my life:
and I will dwell in the house of the Lord for ever"

Psalm 23 (KJV).

A Bridge Over Troubled Water Is Dedicated To:

RocDeeRay

"Talk is cheap, as walking on two left feet. Nonetheless, I've learned to be quiet as I trod down paved asphalted streets. Thank You God for walking alone with me in quiet and in stillness; therefore, there's no need to walk as I speak. I'll let "HIS" shoes speak for me."
Author Renee' Drummond-Brown

Dedicated to: *size 9's (THAT BE ME)!*

"Renee' (Nana)
Spending life with you and watching your growth have been absolutely remarkable. I was so busy watching you from sun up to sundown, raising your family and taking time out to help with others, until, I didn't think you would have enough energy to find your own passion for what you are now doing and that is writing poetry, in an unusual unique way. Your messages touch my every soul. Being a senior citizen, I can appreciate your style of writing and thinking about so much that I missed out on by not paying attention of the importance of knowing the mystery of our history. Thank you for bringing us up to date. It's never too late to learn. Write my child write. Your talent is unmeasurable in what you attempt to do. I am blessed that God gave me you. Proudly, I state this because it is true. You have been my rock; special in every-way. I salute your pure genres of poetry at its best.

Love Mom" (The late Barbara Ann Drummond).

To my late Mother, who has gone home to glory (5-15-2016);
"Mom, I'll forever write the wrongs and be THAT strong bridge over troubled water.
Love Nana" (Renee' Drummond Brown).

A Bridge Over Troubled Water

Other books by Renee' Drummond-Brown:

~TRIED, TESTED and TRUE POETS from ACROSS THE GLOBE
~A B.A.D. Poem
~The Power of the Pen
~SOLD: TO THE HIGHEST BIDDER
~Renee's Poems with Wings are Words in Flight-I'll Write Our Wrongs
And
~e-Book: Renee's Poems with Wings are Words in Flight

Acknowledgements:

Renee Drummond Brown has to be included among the most prolific, pertinent, profound and poetically powerful pen wielders challenging our presuppositions today. She richly rewards every moment you give to taking in her observations on life. I whole-heartedly commend her words with wings to take you over the troubled waters of our times.
Where your treasure is, there your heart will be also.

-Elizabeth Asche Douglas

I love appreciating what is good. Your poetry speaks a lot to me. And as an African who seeks to understand the poetic ideology of blacks in European countries, I embrace the strong voice in your verses, the strength, and the Africanness. Thanks for being a wonderful poet.

-Nnane Ntube

And there is my great poet sister Renee Drummond-Brown.
Your voice dear, is the seeing voice. A voice that speak in colors emphasizing truth, A voice that resonates with love deserved and denied, A voice that puts Godliness first, A voice without fear of saying it as it is, Blessings dear, I/ we applaud your pen, I/ we commend your ink, For the joy of the truth in your lines, Is fearful of creator God, And lessons abide, Amen!!

- Nancy Ndeke-Kenya, Nairobi

You inspire the hearts and minds of a many people and remind me a lot of Dr. Maya Angelou. The sky is the limit for you, I expect even greater things from your future.

-Mark Eggleton

Renee', your work is amazing. Your poetic thought is extraordinary and your use of poetic language is incomparable. Moreover, you tend to leave your readers with a provoking thought.

- Jeffrey Taylor

Ms. Reneé Drummond-Brown approaches her diverse subjects with an expansive vision in her poetic mind's eye, as she weaves together biblical verses, wisdom, humor, solemn thoughts and a unique tenderness about the severe limitations of the lives we live and the times we are in.

Ms. Drummond-Brown's works have been featured on my radio program, Brave New World, on Fifthwall Radio. Additionally, Reneé is a skilled and meticulous reviewer of other writers and has graciously reviewed my own recent book, A Philosophy of Yard, published by Forte Publications.

-Jack Kolkmeyer
Author, Radio Show Host
Fifthwall Radio
Delray Beach, Florida

Renee always awes me with her ability to perceive the real world and put that perception into verses. Not a shy poet, her words are daring and her stance before the surrounding world is bold. Her biting tongue doesn't mince words and the lady doesn't tiptoe when truths must be told. As an editor, I always rub my hands with glee whenever one of her submissions falls into my lap. Her crisp tone brings light into my day and definitely contributes to the number of people who click on the link of our on-line magazine. Do I recommend her poetry? That shouldn't even be asked. Read it and you won't be sorry. Her verses open eyes and minds and warm souls. I do admire this lady of the contemporary poetry and not only because she is so adroit with her writing. She is one of the authors who seek to help others and enriches the contemporary literary world.

-Roxana Nastase
Editor-In-Chief
Scarlet Leaf Publishing House

I operate a daily creative arts e-zine, duanespoetree.blogspot.com, which features new, established, traditional, and experimental writers (mainly poets) and other artists from around the world. Renee' Drummond-Brown is one of the frequently appearing popular poets on the site. Her work ranges from Barbie reminiscences to the African-American experience.

-Duane Vorhees
PoeTree Magazine

Renee' Drummond-Brown is an exceptional poet. She has a signature way of scribing her words that are a must read. She has been a backbone contributor to Raven Cage Zine, a poetry and prose magazine, since the *first issue. Raven Cage has now been in distribution monthly for 2 years. It is hard to imagine the magazine without her.*

- Jerry Langdon
Editor of Raven Cage Zine

Renee Drummond-Brown is an awesome Poetess, writes straight from her Heart and Soul and is very powerful in her verbiage. She has accomplished a great deal, has won multiple awards and I'm glad to say I've given her an award as well from my group POTPOURRI POETS. I enjoy this writer who is a spokeswoman for this Century ...... she's up and coming and making a grand name for herself and is respected highly in the Poetic Circles that we both are part of and I am proud to know Renee.

-Susan Joyner Stumpf, President and Owner,
WILDFIRE PUBLICATIONS, LLC Magazine

Author Renee' Drummond Brown, is a star, leader and go-getter in the poetic world. She graciously blessed me with her poetry and recipes in my cookbook titled "THE SKINNY ON EATING FRESH." Renee' has the kind of writing style as it relates to poetry and/or whatever she writes that I love. I have followed her for so long now and each day is a joy to read her writings. I can't rave enough about Renee's poetry. I give her five stars on every book she writes. I highly recommend her to everyone.

-Deborah Brooks-Langford,
Vice President of Wildfire Publications
Memphis Tennessee

I just love reading Renee Drummond poems. She is a prolific writer. She shoots straight from the hip. I love it! Thanks you Renee for all you do!

-Miss Rutha Mae Harris of Albany, GA.,
Original Freedom Singer and Civil Rights Activist

What can I say? Renee Drummond Brown has done it again. The ink from her pen definitely never runs dry. Her writing is relevant for the times. Keep sharing your passion.

-Judith Hampton Thompson
Publisher, Metro Gazette Publishing Company, Inc.

Renee' Drummond-Brown's writings are hauntingly excellent.... they have the power to pull you into the moment to let you visualize and experience the writer's words...

-Denise Boozer
Atlanta, GA.

A special thank you and acknowledgements to:

Mr. Richard J. Muzzey of *Wonday* Portrait Studio & Location Photography,
for the photographic gifts and talents contributed to my book. www.wondayportraitstudio.com

Mr. Tim Cobb of TNT Photography, for the photographic gifts and talents contributed to my book.
tnt-photo.com

Mr. Anthony Antonelli and Dr. Renee' Barbara-Ann Brown for the contributed You Tube videography.

Mr. Cardell Nino Brown Jr. and Ms. Raven Chardell Brown of RocDeeRay Productions for the
social media contributions and videography.

Renee's Quotes:

"A spirit knows a spirit and I KNOW YOU WELL."

"At the Cross...at the Cross...is where I first saw the LIGHT. And my burdens? Well their HIStory."

"Blackmen sang while Indians cry in their rain. Cept no-man can see their pain."

"Charity begins at home. No it don't. It begins abroad and then God will bless you and your home."

"Dem slaves wrote me down in history."

"GOT MILK? Be for real. America was raised on MY sweet chocolate filled breast!"

"I don't know IF the sun will come out tomorrow, but, one thing for sure, two for certain; The Son will come out and lesson our breast-load of sorrows."

"I SEE you, my sister. I HEAR you, my sister's. But most importantly, I KNOW that I KNOW you, my sistah. A spirit knows a spirit and I KNOW you well!!!"

"If I don't sit at the table; who's gonna teach 'em manners?"

"I'Z gonna flap my black wings till heaven an' earth SANG."

"Less is so much more-sometimes."

"Maya, "STILL I WRITE, I WRITE, I'LL WRITE."

"Our Queens Crowns have been reduced to mere tiara's."

"Peace be still.... AND IT SHALL BE...as it once was!"

"Silence has fought and won some of my best battles."

"Strength is in weakness."

"Talk is cheap; blessings are free."

"The slaves had the right to remain silent and I have the 'write' to speak for them."

"To be or not to be free in the 21st century; education is the answer that will define thee."

"Wherever the Father orders my pen; there goes I Lord!"

"There's Power in my pen; signed Renee' Drummond-Brown."

Renee's Rhythm and Poetic Blues Category:

A BRIDGE OVER TROUBLED WATER

By: Author Renee' Drummond-Brown

You children, without a shadow of doubt;
WILL listen to me,
as I have listened tenderly, and
been taught by the best of the prolific best yet:
Dunbar,
Hughes,
Angelou,
Wheatley, Walker, and
Toi Derricotte. My poetry
links the bridge that connects
unto this 21st century.

My structures' built ov'r
troubled waters.
Erected in Jim Crow's of valley lows,
so others, can continuously cross ov'r me.
To much is given…
much is required.
This. Without a shadow of A doubt is wisdom.
I do know.

A centuries soulful connection. A catalyst,
(if you will). I am thee. My poetries
expose untold
secrecies.
My bridge secures worldviews;
governing a body of international
Civil Rights yesteryears blackISH
kind-of blues.

Moreov'r, my new strength's length
suits any weight
from scholarly to laymen views.

For so long coloreds
have been stripped of dignity,
their voice-tress legacy.
And-yes...shameful to say,
even their exposed lying history.

On 'dat Auction Block;
'dem slaves, could not talk.
So. I come, in the name
Of The Father, Spirit
an' Their Son; POECTICALLY CORRECT.
To spit them sum long, loong, looong
over-due RESPECt.
Don't ever burn that bridge!
And please never forget!
I'll write the wrongs, or
Renee's Poems with Wings are Words in Flight
don't come out
AT ALL!

Dedicated to: 'DEM DEAR SLAVES

A B.A.D. Poem

A Quiet Storm

By: Author Renee' Drummond-Brown

Seen it all
A patsy.
Taking their blame
A patsy.
Taking their falls
A patsy.
Been through it all
A patsy.
A Quiet Storm in their fog
A patsy.

A quiet storm;
devoted-peace that surpasses
their understanding.
Them-boisterous rains are everlasting;
accidents (for them) JUST waiting to happen!

Rain, rain come what may;
'imma bridge who
carries deadmens' weight!
And just like THAT bridge ov'r
troubled waters;
I no longer lay me down,
but'll walk tall with pride hereafter;
for all to still USE an' stand upon
my giant shoulders.

Seen it all
A Quiet Storm.
Taking their blame
A Quiet Storm.
Taking their falls
A Quiet Storm.
Been through it all
A Quiet Storm.
A patsy in their fog
A Quiet Storm.

Gave-em my all
A Quiet Storm.
Answered those beckoned calls
A Quiet Storm.
And they burned the bridge that 'fed-em
while chortling at the repairs.
Still yet, I lay me down to be USED an' walked upon;
year after their year... after their year.

Dedicated to: *Didn't it rain children?*

A RocDeeRay Production

6

ABORT THE MISSION

By: Author Renee' Drummond-Brown

Black and Dehumanized=BAD.
He entered this world with his birthday suit on.
A noose wrapped round his neck (so BAD)
fighting to get here...Dr's., QUICKLY suggest
*mam, please **ABORT THE MISSION...***
PLEASE! Momma protests...
Hell to the naw! Save my unborn!
Save 'em! And I mean right NOW!

In times such as these
'outta concern for them black mommas' bodies

for no reason nor rhymes'
hysterectomies were performed.
'Lookin back in hindsight
genocide for us took its flight!

At birth doctors saw a thug,
obnoxious and loud.
Dad, mom and grans' saw an innocent black-baby-boy
and were lovingly proud!

Just as sure as Renee's poems with wings took flight;
genocides of the 60's were planned like a thief under the knife.
To 'them babies that didn't survive…
MISSION ACCOMPLISHED! Bye bye
Blackbirds'…Bye.

Dedicated to: *MISSION ACCOMPLISHED!*

A B.A.D. Poem

ACE. OF SPADE.

By: Author Renee' Drummond-Brown

*I AM BLACK
LIKE THE
ACE. OF SPADE.
NUMERAL UNO
IF YOU PLEASE.
DID YOU NOT CATCH WHAT HE CREATED
OUT OF THE RAW MINERALS WITHIN ME;
HIS EARTH, HIS QUEEN,
HIS NUMERAL UNO SPADE.*

*I AM MORE THAN JUST
YOUR MERE SLAVE.
NUMERAL UNO
IF YOU PLEASE.
DID YOU NOT CATCH WHAT HE CREATED
OUT OF THE RAW MINERALS WITHIN ME;*

HIS EARTH, HIS QUEEN,
HIS NUMERAL UNO SPADE.

I HOLD AMERICA'S TRUTHS'
TO BE EVIDENT
FROM MY BLACKEST
OF BLACKEST BREAST.
~~~
*NEVERTHELESS,*
~~~
THE WHITEST OF WHITEST
MILK, HOLDS MANY CARDS CLOSET
TO MY CHERISHED TREASURE
OF AN EMPTY TREASURED CHEST.
~~~
*THEREFORE,*
~~~
THEIR
CHILDREN'S
CHILDRENS'
CHILDREN;
'KNOW'
~~~
*THAT THEY KNOW*
~~~
THIS SPADES SUCKLING
WITHOUT ANY HINDRANCE
OF SHAME.

I'M TOO LEGIT TO QUIT
GIVING AMERICA
THE BEST OF MY PUREST BEST
(milk and honey)
YET.

O' CALCIUM, PROTEIN

AND THE SWEETEST
BLACKEST, BERRIED NUTRIENT;
INGREDIANTS DIVINE.
HAND MADE CREATION;
AFFIRMATIVE
FOR MOTHER EARTH
BY NON-OTHER THAN
THE 'ACE'.
FOR
HIS
NUMERAL UNO
SPADE.

WITHOUT
FURTURE ADO
OF EXTENDED SHAME;
I JUST CAUGHT IT
THE KING IS THEE ACE.
OF
THE
SPADE.

Dedicated to: *UNO.*

A B.A.D. Poem

"I am black,
but comely,
O ye daughters of Jerusalem,
as the tents of Kedar,
as the curtains of Solomon.
Look not upon me,
because I am black,
because the sun hath looked upon me:

11

my mother's children were angry with me;
they made me the keeper of the vineyards;
but mine own vineyard have I not kept"
Song of Solomon 1:5-6 (KJV).

Against the Winds

By: Author Renee' Drummond-Brown

A leaf blows
against the winds.
Up, down; to an' fro.

Sometimes shaken
while colors changing.
BUT never is she broke.

Adapts, overcomes,
an' bends
against all probabilities,
BUT not limited to the winds.
(Didn't it rain children? Didn't it?)

Dedicated to: *Airstreams*

A RocDeeRay Production

Ain't Got Nothin' But Pride

By: Author Renee' Drummond-Brown

Stolen from
my Mother land.
Boats sailed me to the Indian land.
Bible 'say'ze' it's da' Promised land.

I question why? Why 'you'ze' hate me so?
Ain't got nothin' but pride.
Heads held on high.
Chin to 'da' sky.
Don't think I'm better than.

Ain't got nothin' but pride. And I walk witta' strut.
Swayin' deze' big boned hips.
Pep in my step...cornbread, collards N' hamhocks' to blame
for ALL OF DIS'.

Arrogance claims my face.
Uppity-ness is what it is.
I can't escape pure grace.
I'z come from
diamonds, salt an' gold.
Iron, cobalt, copper, silver of old.
Petroleum, cocoa beans, wood
and Ohhh'...tropical fruits that ONE cannot hide!

Ain't Got 'Nothin' but Pride.
Don't hate me cause I'z smiles from "YOUR" sea to shining seas.
This' lands y'OUR' land??? No dog in dis' fight!

Ain't Got 'Nothin' but Pride.
I'z come from Kings and Ethiopian Queens.
Remember Sheba??? Solomon's love, SURELY can't hide (t)his'
"BLAAACK"
sustah's pride.
He loved her waaaaaaay back then, and STILL dotes' on her again. AND...
throughout my created plight...
Ain't Got Nothin' But Pride.

THATS' WHY...
My heads'
held
on high!!!

Dedicated to: *Sistah's walkin' tall and carrying a big stick.*

A B.A.D. RocDeeRay Production

ALL God's Childrens'
Ain't Got "Heavy" Shoes!

By: Author Renee' Drummond-Brown

*God placed His heavy weight
in my shoes. Therefore,
"my feet's" and I, shall not, be moved.
Nor complain. The eyelids of my shoes
remind me, to watch, fight, and pray.*

*The tongue of my shoe
is but a two-edged sword.
Speaks volume! Cuts going in!
AND...coming out for sure.*

*My shoes' inner sole
remind me to love the Lord God with all my heart.
With all my mind. And, with all my soul!*

The shoe's heel remind me, to not see
the plagues that surround me,
nor the valley lows or mountain-tops before me.
BUT rather,
look to the hills from which "MY" help comes;
which is, the Father God (within me).

The 2-tied loops, lacing my shoes
touts' a knot, and is but, a threefold cord.
The cord represents the noose
and the knot remind me: THAT...
I WEAR SOME HEAVY SHOES 'fo sho!

ALL God's childrens' ain't got heavy
shoes to bear!
I wear a size SLAVERY
What size 'YOU' wear?

Dedicated to: *"my Momma," who taught me how to 'watch',*
fight and pray. I miss you B.A.D.

A B.A.D. Poem

ANGRY BLACK WOMEN

By: Author Renee' Drummond-Brown

ANGRY BLACK WOMEN

WHO made you so mad?

ANGRY BLACK WOMEN

WHAT if anything; can make you glad?

ANGRY BLACK WOMEN

WHERE are your children, and is that why you're so sad?

ANGRY BLACK WOMEN

WHEN did you give up on the **GOD** that you once had?

ANGRY BLACK WOMEN

WHY don't you try to pray; and maybe your life won't be so bad?

ANGRY BLACK WOMEN

HOW is your life now; that you've returned home to DAD?

Dedicated to: My hurting sisters out there.

A B.A.D. Poem

Baby

By: Author Renee' Drummond-Brown

Baby, what we 'gone do?
I'm 'feedin for two.
Our parents, don't know bout
me an' you.

You're white as the day's long.
I'm black as the night.
Are we so wrong? Or, are they right?

Baby,
what we 'gone do
bout us
3
???

Dedicated to: *How far long are you?*

A B.A.D. Poem

Bad boyz' bad boyz' what cha gone do?

By: Author Renee' Drummond-Brown

Hangin-round about ghetto's town!
Shhh! Lights, camera, action! CUT!
Bout to lose my mind with these nuts!
Seen a lot of poor sons go down!

Sangin' on them corners to gals!
Pimps, prostitutes, Po-Po's on prowl!
Holla! Best circus act around!
Seen a lot of poor sons go down!

Mommas 'feelins preyed on my mind!
Prayers reaching this heart of mine!
Black IZ' the new colour of clowns!
Seen a lot of poor sons go down!

Didn't know my life, be so blue?
Wars and rumors of wars were true!
Gotta' 38 with live rounds!
Ghetto's SCENE all them sons go down!

Dedicated to: *You're under arrest. Anything you say WILL be used against you!*

A RocDeeRay Production

BLACK CRIMES MATTER!

By: Author Renee' Drummond-Brown

Double 'dutchin.
She minds her B I business;
jus-a 'jumpin.

Grey skies.
Green money.
Silver grillz.
Gold chains.
Black asphalt.
White sheet.
Blue rhymes.
Yellow tape.
Red blood.
Glad she ain't mine!
(I never knew double 'dutchin was such a crime)?

She minded her B I business;;
jus-a 'jumpin..
Double 'ducthin..

Grey skies.
Green money.
Silver grillz.
Gold chains.
Black asphalt.
White sheet.
Blue rhymes.
Yellow tape.
Red blood.
Glad she ain't mine!
(I never knew double 'dutchin was such a crime)?

Daddy's 'cryin.
Momma's 'PREYin.
Grandma's 'hate-in.
Wrong man locked up.
I'm 'jus 'sayin...
I never knew double 'dutchin was such a crime??
Glad she ain't mine!!
DO WE MARCH OR TURN OUR HEADS; AT THIS TIME?

Dedicated to:
She had the right to jump silent. And 'everythang shot will still be used against her.

A RocDeeRay Production

BLACK PANTHER

By: Author Renee' Drummond-Brown

*STAY WOKE **BLACK PANTHER** STAY WOKE!*
*Rise **black** cat(s) RISE!*
*Hey you, mr. **BLACK** hunter-man,*
birthed from these tribes
Javan, Sri-Lankan, Indian, Indochinese and African.
By 'faaar, Mother Africa touts
the best of the best, fur coats alive!

Copyrighted colours etched into Eden's infallible grounds. And 'her cats
are everything that I stand for and 'evrythang that I am.
*Rise **black** cat(s) RISE!*
I'M 'STAYIN WOKE!
I'M 'STAYIN ALIVE!!

*STAY WOKE **BLACK PANTHER** STAY WOKE!*
*Rise **black** cat(s) RISE!*
YOU; yeah YOU,
*Mr. **BLACK** cat; lurking round Africa and Asia.*
Arks roaming to 'N fro; onto Mt. Kenya
to the equatorial rain forest of Malaya.
The space you occupy
has the need to breed
'wit the likes of my Negroid lips, broad nose, kinky hair and Afrocentric kind(s).
STAY WOKE!
STAY WOKE!!
I'M 'STAYIN WOKE!
I'M 'STAYIN ALIVE!!

*STAY WOKE **BLACK PANTHER** STAY WOKE!*
*Rise **black** cat(s) RISE!*
***BLACK** CAT, Your melanism*
is the result of the dominant allele
and relatively sets the tone, time and place of your offspring's gene
that "arise" by mutation.
Hey You. Mr. protector, of them cat(s) in the cradle "WITHOUT" a silver spoon.
Teach them to howl
Teach them to howl
at their moons lest they die.
STAY WOKE!
STAY WOKE!!
I'M 'STAYIN WOKE!
I'M 'STAYIN ALIVE!!

*STAY WOKE **BLACK PANTHER**! STAY WOKE!*
*Rise **black** cat(s) RISE!*
Then,
*there's you, Mr. **BLACK** Jaguar-man;*
devious and cunning.
YOU; yes you,
beautiful creature you.
Touting a golden red NEGROID tan.
Marked with tatted rings and spots within,
ALTHOUGH,
"MOSTLY" kept in captivity.
A die-hard cougar's love is 'neva uncertain or wavering!
*STAY WOKE **BLACK PANTHER** STAY WOKE!*
EXTINCTION IS ON THE RISE!
STAY WOKE!
STAY WOKE!
STAY WOKE!!
Lest we die!!!

***Dedicated to:** 'Dem cats out there...#13*
EXTINCTION IS ON THE RISE! STAY WOKE! STAY WOKE!! STAY WOKE!!!

A B.A.D. RocDeeRay Production

"Blacky"

By: Author Renee' Drummond-Brown

Took me to get fifty;
to value my blackened-
buried-juicy-skin. Tis notably pretty.

Naw. 'I'z 'lyin!
Loved, loved, loved 'sum-me,
at the tender-age of twenty!

I shine to the east.
I shine to the west afar.
I shine like God; cause
I'm created in tHis perfect
image...Tar.

Dedicated to:
Sticks and stones will crush one's bones and
"Blacky" lives in the minds-eye forever!

A RocDeeRay Production

Border

By: Author Renee' Drummond-Brown

Don't allow NO
drama, cross your threshold; when one sees' YOU coming,
tell Trouble (capital T)
"get behind me"
YOU gotta be-gone. 'Jus go!

Anytime it shows its ugly face;
it can never be a simplistic hello,
but rather...a hello-BUT...in its place.
Dramas' their first, middle an' last surname,
derived from them OOOL'plantation games. jus the same.

(I know YOU very well). An' YOU wonder why
people don't let YOU in,
or do, the likes of your kind,
kith and kin?

Dedicated to: *Clean up your own dirty house and stay out of others.*

A RocDeeRay Production

Brown's Truth

By: Author Renee' Drummond-Brown

Cut 'em' off at the root
cause a white lie doesn't mean
a brown truth.

Pay attention to what
"they say."
Cause as sure as the day's end;
sins 'foreva sin
and a brown lie has unambiguously
no truth; within.

Dedicated to: *Do you swear to tell the truth, the whole truth and nothing but the truth, so help you God?*

A B.A.D. Poem

Call Me Out My Name Again!

By: Author Renee' Drummond-Brown

Call me what you like.
Call me what you may:
blackie, juju-lips, bald headed cow
and/or, I'll be your slave!
I've answered to it ALL.
Yeah~~~I'll own the disrespect;
within, the blunt of them ignorant blatant calls.
BUT~~~let you get down an' out
hmmmh!!! Blackie, Juju-lips, the bald-headed cow,
and/or Mrs. Slave "WILL" catch you
"WHEN" (not if);
"EVERYTIME" you fall.

Dedicated to: *Us sustah's 'will' show you 'betta than we can tell you!*
Now call me out my name again!!!

A B.A.D. Poem

Colored Gal; How Dare You?

By: Author Renee' Drummond-Brown

Hey you; how dare you smile,
at created designed plans,
snakes injecting your pain(s)
since the beginning O' eden times.
Absolutely, no vaccines can 'ev'r' be re-named
nor immunization. No! not for us;
just overdoses of Μωυσής pain, noah's rain, judas'shame,
absolutely no gains...what a sheer shame?
Lest we forget;
sojourn an' tarry on,
to the back of the bus, wit our very own
dead sons amongst us. An'
remember, neva fo'get,
to teach your kids, 'summadat plagued mess!

Hey you, how dare you smile
when we design, plot, plan an' inject your pain(S).
No vaccinations found...
'EV'R. Nor immunization. No! not for us; colored-gals,
just overdoses...lest we forget
planted in dem-dear 'lyin sons of ours!
but...
sustah's breed on HARD-er fo sho
ALL 'dem dayze long.
no more NATURAL sons
to rob us of. so...half the pains fo US, been LONG gone!
Ain't no chevy to the levy.
nor american pies.
dem levy's been let loose, like
george clinton's
unsung 'songz. 'Nothin but the dawgz in 'em
Why do I feel like that?

Why must I?
pen his rap?

Hey you,
TALKIN TO YOU negro gal,
how dare you; smile
when we designed, plotted, planned while injecting your pain(S).
for self-satisfaction;
'robbin you O' your sons' fo summadat personal gain
for sum-ones' expansion.
Is it you? No not I...
Sounds like Shakespearean language to be or not to be. How
dare you...? And why?

Yes negro-gal... Ms. Saditty; Uppity-you; using that dialect
on the intellect, sumthin, you know nothin bout.
How dare YOU negro-gal
smile?

We'ze smiles cause
YOU
ain't hardly Him.
Signed:
a colored gal
an' her negro friends...

Dedicated to: *a simplistic colored negro-gal like me.*

A RocDeeRay Production

Cut from A Different Cloth

By Author: Renee' Drummond-Brown

Some see them unalike.
My lens views the same.
Although, different mothers;
they share in
on
her last name.

He's fathers pick!
The gal? Well,
you know the drill;
mother openly rejects. She's unquestionably

"The BlackEST Sheep" of the family.

Asymmetrical fabric.
Material an' textile so weak;
just to put this mild...they're both cut
from very different cloths~~~
Ones loved. An' one's
a love child.

Dedicated to: *Step brother(s) and/or sister(s).*

A B.A.D. Poem

Don't Burn Your Bridge!

By: Author Renee' Drummond-Brown

Don't burn your bridges behind you;
erected from a military strategy
that escapes one into retreating
whilst fighting.

One must leave a passage in and out;
in good standing
no doubt!
Cause when you burn that bridge
"burn baby burn"
there's no possibility of turning back!

That bridge makes it viable traversing
one place to another,
so always leave an open door
or pathway, if you will, my brother.

Careful when 'yellin
"burn baby burn,"
cause you've lost future connectivity and
familia-links to cross-one again, or "EVER" return.

Dedicated to: *Don't Burn yOUR Bridge!*

A RocDeeRay Production

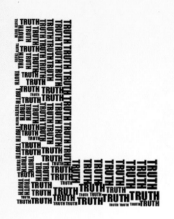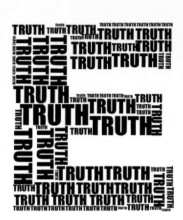

Eye Spy A Lie

By: Author Renee' Drummond-Brown

A good liar tells 90% lies
and 10% truths. He lies,
better than you and/or I do. A great liar, lies
only when needed too. An expert lies
in a court of law to a monetary tune. A bad liar
tells the truth every-time he opens his mouth or whenever
he's forced, to place his right hand on the Cannon's truth.
For ITS rule of thumb is both foretelling and forth-telling and will NEV'R lie
to me or you! Therefore, I swear to tell you the truth,
the whole truth

an' nothin but the poetic truth.
So help me
god!

Now.
Which is the lie an' which is the truth in my poetic scheme of things written down
JUST
for you?

Dedicated to: *Liar, liar, y'OUR' pants are on fire!*

A RocDeeRay Production

Fatigued

By: Author Renee' Drummond-Brown

All our lives us colored gals been attacked, raped, an' hacked. Been called
ev'rythang, BUT... the child of God:
Negro, black, napped, ugly, bald and fat. And you know this;
this is fact! So.
What do you thank' we care bout' lil' ol' you
doin' us in too? Never forget this...
When we are weak,
we are mightier than you!

"Therefore I take pleasure in infirmities, in reproaches, in necessities, in persecutions, in distresses for Christ's
sake: for when I am weak, then am I strong"
2 Corinthians 12:10 (KJV).

Dedicated to: *When a colored gal grows weary WATCH OUT she becomes Mandinka strong!*
"I'm sick and tired of being sick and tired" (Civil Rights Activist Fannie Lou Hamer).

A RocDeeRay Production

Fragile Handle with Care (CRACKED up)!

By: Author Renee' Drummond-Brown

Just shut up!
Save them WOES its me's. An' get off them sheets
an' onto your own two feet. No one owes you
Nothin! Not a thang!! Nor a pillow or comforter
to sleep!!! You. Yes you
'walkin round so dejected, rejected an' totally disrespected, as such;
putting all your trust into needles, bottles and other quote-un-quote victims lying gossip!
They ain't gotta pot to piss in an' you ain't gotta door to throw it out!
But somehow, they got your BACK,
answers, praise and shouts!

In spite of the Cannons' directions.
Some get off, the straight an' narrow.
Then search out; quote-un-quote victims
'inna worse mess of sorrows;
AKA crabs in a wheelbarrow.
I gotta hunch momma warned against such?
STOP. LISTEN! LOOK in the mirror an' ask ones-self
"mirror, mirror on the wall, what 'IZ it, that I'm contributing to my wrongs?"
She'll crack up an' truthfully sang "My chile, birds of a feather, do in fact,
flock together and fools choose fools no matter what the weather. Conditions.
You know what it do? Get a raincoat, galasions, AND a good umbrella too.
Then sang like a temptation
"I got sunshine on a cloudy day; and when it's cold outside"....
"I WISH it was the month of May."

Just shut up!
Save them WOES its me's. An' get off them sheets
an' onto your own two feet. No one owes you
Nothin! Not a thang!! Nor a pillow or comforter
to sleep!!! You. Yes you
walkin round so dejected, rejected an' totally disrespected, as such;

41

putting all your trust into needles, bottles and other quote-un-quote victims lying gossip!
They ain't gotta pot to piss in an' you ain't gotta door to throw it out!
But, somehow, they got your BACK,
answers, praise and shouts!

Dedicated to: *Broken glass; FRAGILE...cracked!*

A B.A.D. Poem

I Am Woman; Hear 'Me' Roar!

By: Author Renee' Drummond-Brown

"And the Lord God caused a deep sleep to fall upon Adam,
and he slept:
And he took one of his ribs,
and closed up the flesh instead thereof;
And the rib,
which the Lord God had taken from man,
made he a women,
and brought her unto the man"
Genesis 2:21-22 (KJV).
The woman's
template
began
something
from nothing
from
the great
I AM;
THAT I AM.

But
she didn't always
follow
the Father's
instructions,
an' because
of this
she'll forever
be
reminded
through
birth
contractions.

The first
woman
began
'our' roar
when she
birthed
'that' very
firstborn,
LEST WE FORGET
CAIN.

Other children
are born
at times
such
as these;
leaving
the woman
torn
with guilt
and
scorn.

Her children
grow
and take
their love
away.
In pity,
she's damaged
goods
and
will forever
morn!
Disrespect,

44

rain,
shame and pain
will attach
to
womanhood.
Often
leaving her
ridiculed
lied on
and
completely
misunderstood.

Her service goes
without
questioning;
which includes
intense
labor of love
pains.
For the rest
of her days,
she gives
of herself
freely
for absolutely
no
personal gain.
Sacrifice
becomes
her signature name.

The Creator
designed her
well,
to tarry on

and
'feed'
His lands.
What
a masterpiece
created
in her
'breast'
from
the great,
I AM
THAT I AM.

The gardens rooted
an'
intriguing woman,
and she,
begot me
down to you.
Firmly
implanted
securely
in rich dirt;
The Father
knew
just
what to do.

Ecclesiastes
gives her
time
to neither
sleep
nor
snore.
Look closely

at
my growth;
I Am Woman;
Hear 'Me' Roar!

Dedicated to: *My 'Roaring Sister's' of all Nationalities.*

A B.A.D. Poem

I Know Why The Caged Byrd Sangs

By: Author Renee' Drummond-Brown

She sangs
cause
she's gotta sermon
in her heart.

She sangs
cause
she's first
not last
at the end
of her bitter start.

She sangs
cause

her virtuous grace
mercies her
a savory song
to sang.

She sangs
cause
slav'ry's
weight of wrongs
scaled her
sympathetic songs
to sing wounds away.

YEAH,
that's why
that NEGRO byrd
sangs.

She sings
cause
tree's swinging
free-men
spared
her only son
from swangin.

Lawd, Lawd, Lawd,
have mercy! The lady sangs
THE BLUES. Yes Lord,
she sings.

She sangs
cause
dem Judas'
is in her way
fills her life with plantation strain~~~

She's gotta cry sumtime
'den
and only 'den
'dat caged byrd
still gotta sang.

She sangs
cause
she's gotta sermon
she brangs.

She sangs
cause she's remains
a Proverbs 31 woman
in her grandiloquent storms
and boisterous rains.

Yeah,
her cup overfloweth
filled 'wit the fruit
of Another's Spirit
an 'dem Songs of Solomon's songs sung
she sangs cause she's gotta sermon
in her colored breast.
And then sum.

That caged byrd
MOANS
her song(z)
to
The Man upstairs
cause you know who
can't translate nor interfere
'wit her melancholy tune
midair.

Maya,
THAT'S WHY
that caged Byrd sangs 'wit His grace,
an' her healthy fear.

Dedicated to: *The late Dr. Maya Angelou. I now know why I sang!*

A B.A.D. Poem

I'LL SAY IT LOUD! I'M BLACK AND I'M PROUD!!

By: Author Renee' Drummond-Brown

Born down South (never free).
Jim Crow knows me by name
YEZZ-mam.
North Carolina,
still swings us on poplar trees.

Silenced to a system.
Seated in the back of them classrooms.
Only to be spoken WHEN spoken to.
Knowing the rules, a colored gal like me;
YEZZ-mam,
should've 'neva been introduced
to anybody's poetry.

'Walkin while being black
YEZZ-mam.
Unlike you, Iz' 'gotta FEAR
for me and my family's life!

A two-edge blade
YEZZ-mam,
just the same (what a shame?)
I gotta WATCH them AND fight my own
slaves. All-the-while playing in these ruthless games!

So, I got the right to be mean.
YEZZ-mam.
The right to fight.
YEZZ-mam.
The right to not care AND be seen.
YEZZ-mam.
The right to not be so nice.
YEZZ-mam.
I ev'n have the right to contest
your ill-wills while harboring legit feelings
inside me until you decide to live up to your creed.

Therefore,
I'LL SAY IT LOUD!
YEZZ-mam!
I'M BLACK AND I'M PROUD!!

Dedicated to: *Stepin' fetchit.*

A RocDeeRay Production

53

'Ima Colored Girl

By: Author Renee' B. Drummond-Brown

'Ima colored girl,
who hides her smile. All the while
sometimes late. But always on time.
'Ima colored girl,
who holds her past.
Make no bones 'bout it. I'll take you on a swirl.
But I know that I know that I know. The first will be last
and the last will be first.
'Ima colored girl,
who wears a mask;
Maya and Paul Laurence Dunbar
said, it's OK to grin 'n hide,
but whateva' you do
bear that tide.
'Ima colored girl,
I WEAR MY SWAG.
Naps 'n all,
braids down my back,
expensive-weave bought at the mall.
'Ima colored girl,
ash claim my knees, crust own my feets'
but when cleaned up (Hmh),
YOU 'betta ask somebody 'bout ME!
'Ima colored girl,
I even have a song
'Lawd have mercy, Marvin Gaye,

"Lets get it on."
'Ima colored girl,
I don't need your acceptance;
cause
'Ima colored girl.
And that ain't what you was expecting!

Dedicated To: *Renee' (Dee-Dee) and Raven (Blackbird) You Black Girls Rock!*

A RocDeeRay Production

London Bridge Is Falling Down

By: Author Renee' Drummond-Brown

Bridge the gap with all your friends.
Remember, 'never-ev'r 'do-em in.
Once that bridge
comes tumbling down.
You'll never walk-cross, it, again!
I've 'seen-em come 'and-go with a frown;
'an-attempt return,
with
an up-side-down frown drawn. When all along,
their bogus smile's,
merely, London Bridge, 'falling-down!
Again, 'never-ev'r 'do-in 'a-friend.

Cause once that bridge comes tumbling down;
you'll 'never-ev'r
'cross-it again!

Dedicated to: *Toll please (the price of friendship)!*

A RocDeeRay Production

Long Live the Queen ARETHA FRANKLIN

By: Author Renee' Drummond-Brown

"A NATURAL WOMAN"
with love, "R.E.S.P.E.C.T" and honor who
sang "A LITLE PRAYER"
to a "CHAIN OF FOOLS."
"I KNEW YOU WERE WAITING"
so, "DON'T PLAY THAT SONG"
leaving us to "THINK"
"SINCE YOU'VE BEEN GONE."
"AIN'T NO WAY"
I'm gone "ROCK STEADY"
on this "FREEWAY OF LOVE"
"UNTIL YOU COME BACK TO ME."
We be "DAY DREAMING"
Ree-Ree, "BABY I LOVE YOU"
"DO RIGHT WOMAM, DO RIGHT"
cause THEE...DR. "FEEL GOOD" now has you

taking HIS flight,
"SOMETHING HE CAN FEEL"
that's so very Divine and right.

Yesteryear's, she sang us a love song that we so choose,
but, on this very day 8-16-2018, Aretha declares,
"I SING "GOD" THE BLUES."

Dedicated to: *Until you come back to me that's what I'm 'gonna do!*

A RocDeeRay Production

My Best Isn't Good Enough

By: Author Renee' Drummond-Brown

I gave ALL I had to give.
And yet...
All in all, I saw no return.
My "VERY" best wasn't good enough
(for you).
I guess?

Dedicated to: *Lack. Or there of?*

A RocDeeRay Production

60

Negronis' We Get You

By: Author Renee' Drummond-Brown

BROTHER'S we get you. AND,
WE forgive you.. You had but only ONE
THAT you could do in. AND,
THAT was the 'coloured woman and her children. Brother's, we love us some you. AND,
WE forgive you. Because we of all people KNOW;
THE PURE HELL you've been put through. We're sorry that we stopped believing in YOU.
WE'RE sorry that we gave up on you. BUT...
YOU gotta do your PART
MUCH better; on 'lovin on us TOO.

Dedicated to: *From 'sum hurt sustahs' to our Kings.*

A B.A.D. Poem

Nowhere Ov'r the Rainbow

By: Author Renee' Drummond-Brown

Somewhere over the rainbow
A bluebird did fly.
But…
for a colored girl like me,
'da wounded Raven-bird lies.
Her wings cover
a multitude of sin. Come out; come out
wherever you are. But NO, not her.
She'd rather hide cause
nowhere 'Ov'r 'THAT' rainbow
does a black colored girls' fairytale fly.

Dedicated to: *Broken blackbirds don't fly, they hide…*

A B.A.D. Poem

Phillis Wheatley

By: Author Renee' Drummond-Brown

Born in West Africa, 1753;
died at the tender-age of 31,
Boston Massachusetts, you see,
claims-her rich-blood.
But. What she did in-between
was Master to none-other, than, those poetic writes' she
so eloquently inked.

Seized from Senegal/Gambia, West Africa,
incarcerated at merely 7 years of age.
Crossing the Atlantic (all by herself)
'po 'lil colored-gal, packed 'inna-cargo of exiled negro slaves.
Entering an exit-door of no return.
Transported to Boston-docks in
a sealed slave-ship called The Phillis;
owned by none other than Timothy Fitch and Peter Gwinn
My Lord! What a sight unseen for this
innocent childs' harsh begins?

More deadly
than alive on arrival;
this pint-size literati
was sold to Mr. John Wheatley.
The highest bidding wealthy-
merchant tailor-man;
purchasing this negro-gal
for his wife Susanna and
of-course, surnaming her, Phillis
after that slaveships' battles within thee;
tossing her to an' fro

against an assaulted angry sea;
as she mentally penned to her-God
"Lawd, why ain't You come see bout me?"

Wouldn't you know? He'd
land her in America; the home of them braves'
that purchased-her 'fo-free.
The Wheatleys' solidified-her a-slave.
In addition, to giving Wheatley
Americas' transPARENT shame.

Their daughter and son
taught Phillis reading, writing and then some.
But God, gets all the glory, honor and praise!
For tHis act; un-beknowing to the Wheatley's...
was preordained by "His" Only Begotten Son!

By 12 this genius was already reading
Greek and Latin
and 14, her first poetic write was already written
to the University of Cambridge,
in New England.

Her genre couriers' feelings and ideas
capturing the use
of figurative language and forfeits the vessel;
silently exposing them ships and its ruse-
tactics of treasured Mandinka warrior wrestlers.
Her genre of literature raises questions in today's muse
as well as the hereafter...

Her literary work still echoes with special concentration;
concentrating on distinctive subject matter of a slave;
slaves bridging Africa to America's enslaved;
enslavement linking me back into her genre of chains;
chains that connect to America's 21st century refrains;

refrains resounding the very first blacks' publications;
publications of thangs that have yet to change;
change that wants to make America great again;
again, the more colored thangs change the more they stay the same;
same ol' me, re-sounding like Phillis Wheatley;
Wheatley's eighteenth-century bridge ov'r troubled water still remains;
remains in me.

Dedicated to: *Phillis Wheatley; the very first African American to publish a book and achieve intercontinental attention as an author.*

A RocDeeRay Production

POETRY

By: Author Renee' Drummond-Brown

Poetic thoughts
Outweigh
Eternity
Time
Re-writes
Yesterday

Dedicated to: *Poetic thoughts running through the corners of my mind.*

A B.A.D. Poem

Raccoon

By: Author Renee' Drummond-Brown

I'm tired of sangin
songs sung
in them fields.

I rather be hung
from the highest poplar tree;
than pick a bale
O' cotton. Real talk. Now that's for real!
So, you see...

You can always tell a raccoon
by his/her face. A gentle mask
worn. A ringed tale. The best
fur coat on. Hiden
'inna'
crowded room,
NOTICEABLY
out of place!

Sporting a two-tone face; greyish-brown.
Made in America. Let's call this poem
EXACTLY what it is. A spade is a spade is a spade!
Now be for real; cause
a man of wisdom assuredly knows
the real deal!

Dedicated to: Perpetrators.

A B.A.D. Poem

Still I Write (The Answer to: Dr. Maya Angelou's "Still I Rise")

By: Author Renee' B. Drummond-Brown

Maya,
Of course,
they wrote you down
in history.
You proved
them wrong
in truth.
But you
planted for me
calligraphy.
So,
I'm heard on paper
all the way
to God's celestial roof!
My passion for writing
does upset them.
But
I can't be
concerned.
Cause you
left for me

a gift from God.
And it'll be
forever
writing that I yearn.

Just like God's Raven
leaving the Ark.
'She' flew
to and fro.
Until the waters
were dried up
from off the earth.
Because of you,
I'll forever
write
in the skies,
seas
and dirt;
for certain
this
I do know.

I was
that broken soul.
And bowed
so low
to Satan's pit.
With nowhere
to get;
but up.
I allowed my pen
to place me
within God's Script (ure).
I know
my writings
excite you.

And with God
for you,
who can be
against us,
in giving me
that nod?
I finally hear
your words
loud and clear;
the poems you left behind
are messages
of truths,
minus
the facades.

Some have
shot my writings
to pieces.
While others
have damaged me
over time.
But God;
sends a ram
in a bush,
ink,
a quill,
and wrote for me
Ecclesiastes 3.
He Author's
the time and place
with limited 'seasons'
for their
hurtful rhymes.
From the shame
you told me to write,
I write.

From the pain
you told me to write,
I write.
I am
that Raven Blackbird
with a large wingspan.
"Renee's Poems with Wings are Words In Flight;"
flying all over
God's land.
I too
want to leave behind
my unhealthy fears.
So,
in the dark,
I write.
But in the light,
I see
the imagery
our ancestors gave
to you;
which you
passed onto me.
Maya,
you are the dream,
Barack Obama
was the hope,
and I
am the slave set free
(to write).
Still I write.
I write.
I'll write.

Dedicated to: *Dr. Maya Angelou's memory and lifetime of grind.*

A B.A.D. Poem

Titanic

By: Author Renee' Drummond-Brown

Tired is as tired does. She floats on
carless streams; who knows no love. She floats on river-banks
giving her all to the poor. She floats on oceanic "blues"
of a dark history's past
"SEEshores" + "SEEshells" - white beaches = black quicksand. She's
not built to last. Duracell, ALKALINE and Energizer
keeps her going and going and going. CHARGE-she's gone!

Can't you "sea?" The saltwater pressures her blood
greater than the strength of them waterfalling hearts. She boils!
She boils!! She boils!!! And can't hide!
But why?
Ain't no pearls clamed inside. Can't you "sea?"
Her lake's shallow and parliament knee deep. They can't
swim like she
and never did; they learn. Can't you "sea?"

Her army, her navy, her coastguard are the few, were the proud,
but in no way can withstand alone without THE marine!

Walking by faith
gets momma utterly exhausted for which she terminates
the struggle for them quote-un-quote
un-grates.
Forevermore, can she no longer float on
sureSEEs and/or SEEshores; whichever!
BUT
when them momma's give up; WATCH IT NOW!
EVERYONE DROWNS!
and i mean everyone; FOR "SHORE!"
"Their" life jackets will forever work
no-more.

Sending out an' SOS
can't help the raging of an angry battered sea.
Nothin' like a shipwreck
that gets tossed
AND
turns.

Dedicated to: *The heart of the ocean!*

A B.A.D. RocDeeRay Poem

Wisdom Seeds

By: Author Renee' Drummond-Brown

Coming into self-worth.
Worth surly knows my skins wealth.
Wealth covered beneath the earth.
Earth birthed me from Negro dirt.
Dirt housing, I, me, myself.
Myself, me and I now know;
know the skin I'm in magnets growth.
Growth breeds seeds producing wealth!

Dedicated to: *Juju beans*

A B.A.D. Poem

WOMAN

By: Author Renee' B. Drummond-Brown

Good Black don't crack is where my secret lies.
I got junk in my trunk and extra pounds to loan for size. They don't need to know
our tit for tat. But the 30 years between us
means the world and that's that. I am your woman;
Yes indeed.
Maya Angelou defined me as phenomenally.
Why can't that be me?
Ms. Phenomenally?
Nice Ring.
Ms. Phenomenally!
Yes! That's me; indeed. So you see,
don't get it twisted. I'm a soul searching Sistah;
A woman after God's own heart. That's me
Thank you Dr. Maya Angelou,
You described me phenomenally. Yeah. That Woman is me!

Dedicated to: *Dr. Maya Angelou's Phenomenal Women*

A B.A.D. Poem

Xenophobic

By: Author Renee' Drummond-Brown

Racist amongst us
are pen to paper
whilst revulsion is to
haters. As chauvinistic is to bigotry as xenophobia is to
discriminators. Truth be told, prejudices'
plague our nation,
our minds,
our bodies
an' our souls.
Racist amongst us
are pen to paper sketching our ignorance with ONE
Crayola crayon.

Dedicated to: *Odium*

A RocDeeRay Production

Societal Issues Category:

400 Years

By: Author Renee' Drummond-Brown

Father,
What do
the brown momma's do?
Like the Israelites, we keep
crying out for You,
and only for You.

An' then
crying out
again,
an' again,
an' again
and only then; we lament
some more. For our firstborns.

Cause the rest
are EXTINCT!!!

KILLED
in 'dem dear streets!
No more sons to rob us
of~~~.
No more suckling of our breast.
From father like son.

Like Judas, their crossroad inevitably
will be met. By
the measure(s) they meet.

Plenty tags for 'dem toes
from the corners office;
evidence do show.

OH, MY GOD!
'Dem cold, cold, feet(s')!

Don't act like
you don't know
???
Remember
YOU WILL
REAP
WHAT YOU SOW~~~

On 'dis
side of Jordan;
please let my people go?

What
a sick joke
played now,
an' ev'n back then.
But~~~then again,
we're strangers
on Indian land(s).

Land neither owned
by our
family,
foe
nor

79

friend(s).
This land 'AIN'T' ours.
IT'S THEIRS!

O' Israel,
Israel,
what happened to
justUS?

Wondering 400+ years.
Poverty stricken; slaves
more or less.
Premeditated
for us an'
our kin;
in plain view with shame
tornadoes twirling us to an' fro
non-stop thundering rains.
Which way is up?
Down?
Which way do we turn?
Who do we trust?
Where do we go?

Please answer our call.
FOR THE SAKE OF US ALL.

How long?
We've withstood.
How long?
We've withstood.
How long?
We've withstood it all
(I can't stand no more).

No more sons to bury.
Extinction.
We've absolutely no glory, limited faith and hard core love!

Love has returned home
with our sons, including the grace that came and has
long, long-gone. No longer wise as a serpent
nor gentle, as THAT Dove.

How long?
How long?
How long?
We've withstood.
We've withstood.
We've withstood it all.

Colored women left to fend all alone
to tear the FINAL remnants DOWN
until we ultimately destroy what is left
to each of our own.

The word said
this world is without end.

Time to face that music
'sustahs'~~~
400 more years foreign to Thee in this wilderness~~~
just aimlessly
wondering more or less.
No God.
No man.
No sons.
Just US.
Until
we are no more!

Dedicated to: *Lost in space~~~*

A B.A.D. Poem

1961

By: Author Renee' Drummond-Brown

There's a place where trees grow
Not in Oz
though; but rather, up South,
this, I do know.

I've walked there; in the shadow of death
I've feared the evil
at its very best,
yet, 'sum say, I know not what I speak about.

I won't tell you; you already know 'fo real
Civil Rights?
Who am I 'tryin to kid?

And, I won't tell you her name
--anyway. Because we dwell in a society
of Southern comfort that refuses ownership of change
America, America; lady Liberty, shed sum grace.

Dedicated to: *The good 'ol 'dayze ain't been so good*
and the bad 'ol dayze are understood.

A B.A.D. Poem

A, B, C Easy as 1, 2, 3

By: Author Renee' Drummond-Brown

We entered this world crossed off as
A
0.
The 50's and 60's
trained us the
K.K.K
and Jim Crow laws.
But...we held-on to the
+
as our cold bodies swung back and forth.

The educational games

of the 70's, 80's and 90's were/ARE definitely played.
F
surly graded our fate.
Turning us into 'sum ol'
G's.
Assuring us the school to prisons pipeline role.
Next, came systematic parole.
Then, no jobs.
Finally, street-time; roaming-us to and fro.
But God.

Now
X
marks our-spot(S) where we're fatally shot!
But God.

Y
you do us like
U
do?

Careful now, cause
I
heard when
U
dig one ditch
U
better-dig
2,
cause A, B, C's aren't easy as 1, 2, 3.
Who knew 1+1 would be 2 for both me and U?

Dedicated to: *Do-re-mi-fa-sol-la-ti-do.*

A RocDeeRay Production

A Child of God?

By: Author Renee' Drummond-Brown

That
white gal, entered my world
'witta authentic
biracial son.
Through him; she fully cogitates
JUST what it means to be
a black man. In America.
But...
She loves on 'em hard. Anyhow.

But... can't expect her daddy,
of the 50's to forget:
the march
the dream
the hose
the dogs
the NO votes
the lunch counters
the lynching's and most of all
she should count her auspicious stars
she birthed him in the 21st century
an' be EV'R so grateful to God.

Dedicated to: *His eye is on His sparrows and He even watches my 'chillins.*

A RocDeeRay Production

DRUMMOND

And A Child Shall Lead Them?

By: Author Renee' Drummond-Brown

What happened to the fight we once
had within us? What happened to holding on throughout
our midnights? What happened to prayin through those storms,
winds and boisterous rains? Until clear. Out of sight! What happen to lifting our
brothers up? And 'NOT' giving them the drank or the drugs! What happen
to educating our girlz on virtues, cleanliness and boyz? What happen to teaching them, to iron, cook, sew,
clean and their culture? What happen to hiding the Scriptures
in their heart of hearts?
WHERE MY SOLIDERS AT?

HERE WE ARE.
10 years old, livin an dyin on our VERY own. Getting shot as a sport.
Homeless in this thang called "The Hood." A war zone at its best...But. If...there IZ a God??? We've been
passed that test!!! 2 to the head 1 to the chest...Means absolutely nothin in this sick war! Society cares nothin

bout us. A local bridge holds our cots and cups. Another homeless, cares for us. And he got NOTHIN but pity minus sum luv. The news don't report what we have to say. Healthcare at 26, years of age? What a sick joke! WE'RE OUT HERE dyin anyway! Keep it. If it makes you retract and repeal. Keep it. Cause we're the one's in the army now; drafted without consent. Did I say 10 years old? Truth be told I'm 9 taking care of one 7, 6 and five. I think. No birth certificates. I'm in the REAL army now and uncle sam don't even know who I am? Scripture proclaims "And a child shall lead them" (Isaiah 11:6) Well here I am! Behind the veil. Ever so ready to dwell with both wolf and the lamb. Shhh.

Silence of the lamb(S).

The law of the land is evolution that tames the dog..and here I am, a soldier
that didn't ask for this job (AT ALL) and undeniably knows no wrong!
You asked
but do you really want to know, or even care?
HERE WE ARE
we're in y'OUR' army now
10, 9, 8, 7, 6, 5, 4, 3, 2, and 1 year olds.

Dedicated to:
"I believe the children are our future. Teach them well and let them lead the way"
(George Benson).

A RocDeeRay Production

Another one bites the dust... and another one of "US" gone.

By: Author Renee' Drummond-Brown

We lamented in Ramah,
with bitter weeping for our CHILDREN.
HOW LONG?
We refuse to be comforted
because THEY still are not.
HOW LONG?
We refrain our voice and weep tearless eyes.
Has OUR reward been forgot?
HOW LONG?
We brought these KIDS from the land of the enemy
to a promise. Milk & Honey.
HOW LONG?
The land of the FREE
enslaves our CHILDREN'S CHILDREN'S, CHILDREN'S dreams.
HOW LONG?
We so wanted THEM to taste
The Bread of life's Manna.
HOW LONG?

"How long wilt thou forget me, O LORD? for ever?
how long wilt thou hide thy face from me?
How long shall I take counsel in my soul, having sorrow in my heart daily?
how long shall mine enemy be exalted over me" Psalm 13:1-2 (KJV)?

Is there any faith, hope and love left to give THEM?
HOW LONG?
Shall ANY of our CHILDREN be left
to EVER reach Your border?
HOW LONG?
WE'RE TIRED OF 'SANGING
THEM SAME 'OLE SAD SONGS;
Another one bites the dust...
and another one of "US" (POW) gone.

HOW LONG
and how many more
REQUIRED to reach heaven's shores
with heavy shoes on.

But...with every good-bye;
still hope lies
on a promise. We trust.

Dedicated to: *Another one bites the dust... and another one of "US" gone.*

A B.A.D. RocDeeRay Production

BLACK ON BLACK RACISM

By: Author Renee' Drummond-Brown

BLACK ON BLACK RACISM
YES, it exists!
And yet, we're uncomfortable
'talkin bout this...
Let it be known
we've experienced it!
So, truth be told...
I WON'T PLEAD THE 5th
IT DOES IN FACT EXIST.

There's that one, on the job
who gets ahead,
'jumpin in-an-out of 'ev'ryone's bed.
They won't-ev'n give the-likes-of-their-own-kind, a-mere-nod
for fear of losing, their quote-un-quote created job. Instead
they take-on the mentality;
I got mine. Now get your own-bread.

91

BLACK ON BLACK RACISM

YES, it exists!
And yet, we're uncomfortable
'talkin bout this...
Let it be known
we've experienced it!
So, truth be told...
I WON'T PLEAD THE 5th
IT DOES IN FACT EXIST.

And I-ain't, forgot about you Mr. or Mrs., Jealousy;
cause-you refuse to climb the ladder of success
so, you-display the worst type of jealousy. Which is being maliciously-envious!
Throughout that office you plant your brother and sister's-distress;
always putting-em down by bringing up their past
in-an-attempt to turn the tables round with your mess.
Take that dung somewhere else!

BLACK ON BLACK RACISM

YES, it exists!
And yet, we're uncomfortable
'talkin bout this...
Let it be known
we've experienced it!
So, truth be told...
I WON'T PLEAD THE 5th
IT DOES IN FACT EXIST.

And then there's YOU family...One gets ahead,
you pull-em down
and hold-em back; instead
of pushing-em through.
You gather stones and make up lies (too) in them streets
in an-attempt to get the who black community
against the ONE who tries to get ahead
and-onto their-own two-feet.

And when that ONE leaves-home and makes' it
in this cold-cold, world you see;
then we-say "its-a-shame, they-changed
and forgot about-me!"
But I-say, "Did you support their-rap? 'Outta their-car buy their CD's?
Books? Help-raise their-babies? Or did you just, lay-in-state and wait, to hate on thee?
Sit-back, shut-up, and just-wait!
SUPPORT THEM AT THEIR CRAFT!
Maybe. Just maybe. They have a-plan B, that decides the whole families fate!
If you won't-help, jUSt
SIT-BACK, SHUT-UP, AND PRAY!"

BLACK ON BLACK RACISM
YES, it exists!
And yet, we're uncomfortable
'talkin bout this...
Let it be known
we've experienced it!
So, truth be told...
I WON'T PLEAD THE 5th
IT DOES IN FACT EXIST.

Ya'll STOP 'hatin on your-own.
You-ain't hardly there with-them, on those restless-nights.
So-learn to-be-proud of their dreams
when taking flight.
And dreamers, when your-own don't receive you in-your-own home, wipe your-feet
shake their dung from your-heels and 'leave-em
right-there...
with their "black lies" mattering, ONLY to them.

BLACK ON BLACK RACISM
YES, it exists!
And yet, we're uncomfortable
'talkin bout this...
Let it be known

we've experienced it!
So, truth be told...
I WON'T PLEAD THE 5th
IT DOES IN FACT EXIST.

BLACK ON BLACK RACISM
is-a real-twist and truth-be-told;
I-ain't pleading no 5th
because racism hurts "US" against both black and white while trying to grow
out-there all-alone in-the-cold.
Am-I, my brother's down-fall?
Yes! I'm a racist against my own.
jUSt OWN IT ALL
lest we fall.

Dedicated to: *I don't know; is this you? jUSt OWN IT and let the poem do what it do!*

A B.A.D. RocDeeRay Production

Cycles

By: Author Renee' Drummond-Brown

Momma told her not to do IT.
IT was done; she did not LISTEN
LISTEN to her, for what, and why, she too did it, AFTER-ALL?
AFTER-ALL, she had her at 16.
16, she, herself, should've been pristine CLEAN.
CLEAN as bleach on a summers CLOTHESLINE.
CLOTHESLINES, yeah, not soils hung out to DRY.
DRY stains. Tide can't even get these out, nor CAN;
CAN a praise and/or SHOUT!
SHOUT it out!!! Should've been 'playin 'wit dolls, jacks and balls til 9:00.
NINE months to GO.
GO to jail...do not pass go til 18
EIGHTEEN-year BIDS.
BIDS her FAREWELL.
FAREWELL Momma says, "I told you so."

Dedicated to: Recurrences

A RocDeeRay Production

95

EENY MEENY MINY MOE

By: Author Renee' Drummond-Brown

Eeny meeny miny moe
hang a negro
by his throat.
'IF' he 'hollas
don't let 'em' GO;
that's the way
the good ole
American dream
works!

Dedicated to: *PicNICS.*

A B.A.D. Poem

FATHER DEAREST

By: Author Renee' Drummond-Brown

You raised 2 wonderful boys. Played with them
and
their Fao Schwarz expensive toys. Taught em'
to crawl, walk, talk and cogitate. Taught em' to ride bikes, walk trails and go on
long, loong, looong hikes. Walked em'
to school when missing their bus. Pulled out
that very first tooth and such; 'ev'n took em'
for weekly 'costly' haircuts.

Worship and prayer time
was ALWAYS in demand between you
and them. YOU helped em'
with homework; solely responsible for their A's! Even
coached their soccer, basketball, baseball and AAU teams! Drove em'
to their first dance and then taught em'
to drive, before, buying em'
BOTH cars.
GO YOU...

97

FATHER DEAREST. 'YOU' ARE DEFINITELY 'THE' SUPERSTAR
OF SUPERSTARS!

You taught em' to dress. 2 piece,
black double breasted suits; worn down their chest. Sharp
as a tack. Two 6ft. 2 men all dressed
in black. You taught em' to explore,
travel the world and YOU
even went on their individual college tours. You taught em'
to cover up and how NOT to get a girl pregnant!
Whew! Now I'm impressed!!
THAT
IS BOTH
RESPONSIBLE and PO-WER-FUL yet!!!
GO YOU!!!!

You ev'n said grace before they ate. You made
boyz' to men as such.
Great job
STEP-DAD OF THE YEAR!
BUT.
I GOTTA' HUNCH
YOUR BIOLOGICAL "NATURAL" SONS
GOT NONE OF "THAT" TIME NOR YOUR LOVE!
What 'YOU' think; what's up?

Dedicated to: *Go YOU! Clap. Clap. Clap. Clap. Clap. Clap. Clap!*

A RocDeeRay Production

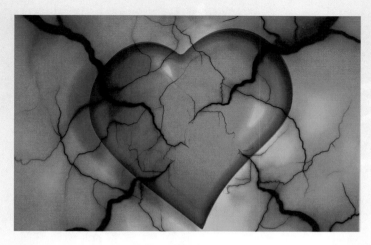

Half Blood

By: Author Renee' Drummond-Brown

*Half me
wanna
be free.
Half me
wanna know
our identity.
Half me
belong
to mommy.
Half me
belongs
to Massa's
genealogy.*

Dedicated to: *Massa; 'nothin' but the blood.*

A B.A.D. Poem

HOW DARE YOU!

By: Author Renee' Drummond-Brown

HOW DARE YOU

say:
we should get 'ov'r
what happened yesterday;
when yesterday, still occurs
today!

HOW DARE YOU

say:
we can't breathe
oxygen supplied
by The One
who gets THE last say!

HOW DARE YOU

say:
hands up don't shoot
is 'jus something we say
'JUST' to have
something to say!

HOW DARE YOU!

Cause last I checked;
'ONLY' brown 'boyz
are 'STILL' being
blown-away legally unto
this very day.

Dedicated to: *How Dare You!*

A RocDeeRay Production

Liberty an jUStice for Sum

By: Author Renee' Drummond-Brown

My ears done been through slavery. My
wise eyes done been through the civil rights movement. My
mouth's been through the 21st century. I pen em'
like I see em' and feels nothin in return. Lady liberty has un-dressed me and
put all my funeral clothes on. Underneath all her mean green is rusted
cobs. She's merely an Ace of Spade 'sportin a callous ball n' chain. jUSt
like me. Although, we're both
rusty round the edge...if truth be told...she's blacker than me.

No man IZ an island. But. Lady liberty
ain't hardly free!

Dedicated to: *Yesteryears, today and tomorrow.*

A B.A.D. RocDeeRay Poem

PREDICAMENT

By: Author Renee' Drummond-Brown

Because we didn't listen
to our Commandments.
We are placed in solitary confinement
within our present condition.
Whereas, the woman
has now turned into the man
and the men now watch the children,
while the woman works
for her boy. All the while the household suffers
and everyone is indelibly hurt;
while staged with technology and extravagant toys.

Dedicated to: *Family.*

A RocDeeRay Production

Same 'Ole Sad Song

By: Author Renee' Drummond-Brown

Critics say racism
doesn't exist
(YEAH RIGHT).
Let 'em try 'walkin
in my BLACK skin a bit.

They'll definitely
'SANG the blues my friend.

And I'll sang a song
for you;
you'll sang a song
for me.
I guarantee
WITHOUT
a shadow of a doubt;
they'll come up outta
my shoes an' SANG
the same ole' sad song;
I once SANG'
to you!

Dedicated to: *Sending out an SOS (Save Our Skin)!*

A B.A.D. Poem

Seasons in the Sun

By: Author Renee' Drummond-Brown

Slavery sorrows synthetic songs.
1619
bothers ABSOLUTELY no-one
at-all. Birth owns negro skin, and
faithful pains are loaned
ov'r an ov'r an ov'r
from within. Again,
a COLORLESS rainbow
for times such as these.

Nonetheless, the logos, the logos
Habakkuk 2:3 boast
"For the vision is yet for an appointed time,
but at the end it shall speak, and not lie."

Yet one's truths' for us coloreds, has re-written
so many lies.
Liar, liar!!! Dem pants on fire!
Yet, time passes us some real
good-byes'.

Are there man-made seasons
in the sun? Or,
are they predetermined
from THAT red oceanic ocean
we rode on?
Or, are they determined
by more lies? That drift on a memory;
with a locked door of no return-address
and/or a-key.

If one's vision is truly appointed within seasonal time;
then our season
has long died before the cries of 1619 cries.

Dedicated to: *What happened to the joy and fun 1619 robbed us of?*
From a colored gals point of view.

A B.A.D. Poem

The Chicken's Finally Came Home to Roost

By: Author Renee' Drummond-Brown

Father God,
my heart cries out
for Antwon Rose;
who can no-longer write for his beloved momma,
poetries of prolific prose.

My heart cries out for his dad, family and grans.
who's weighted shoes
for the rest of their days
are filled
with anger and steadfast blues.

My heart cries out for the community
who's justice served will never brang
Emmett Till's family
understanding that surpasses peace.
REMEMBER them sad sad songs
that we as coloreds
are now forced to sang for Antwon's memories?

My heart cries out for Michael Rosfeld's family
who's bondage
will finally understand
our tormented 400 years of enslaved pleas;
and yet,
we're "STILL" here counting a Kings dreams...

My heart cries out for Malcolm X,
WHO
forewarned us;
what would inescapably happen next.
I guess "JUST"

like X said: aLLLLLLL
"OUR" chicken's finally came home to roost! Father forgive "US"
for we "STILL" know not; what it is "WE" do?

Dedicated to: *Everybody loses.*

A RocDeeRay Production

THE DOOR OF NO RETURN

By: Author Renee' Drummond-Brown

I HATE
DOORS.
I HATE
WINDOWS,
AN'
I LOATHE
TREES.

THE DOOR OF NO RETURN
LOCKED
MY ANCESTORS AND ME OUT
OF EVER
BEING FREE.

THE WINDOWS
I MUST CLIMB THROUGH; FOR
MRS. MISSY;
MY MOMMAS HANDS, SLAVED.
TO KEEP EM CLEAN.

AS FOR DEM
SOUTHERN TREES.
NAW,
I'Z LYING.
~ ~ ~
ALL
TREES BEARING LEAVES;
I'VE HAD TO WATCH
FROM CLEAN WINDOWS,

BEHIND LOCKED DOORS...
MY
COLORED BOYZ
SWING.

Dedicated to: *Mrs. Missy.*

A B.A.D. Poem

We Rode On The Bones Of A Slave

By: Author Renee' Drummond-Brown

We rode
on the bones
of slaves.
To see these 'so called'
sunny days.

That lil' girl
traveled here
'dreamin' 'bout' our world.
Washed ashore
in this land of the free;
home of the brave,
working her 'TAIL'. Literally!

They forgot to tell her
'WHEN'
they stole her away;
'WE'D' forever be
America's Slave(s).

Never again
being freed.
Instead,
she intercedes
for both you and me.
She prayed
some loooooooooooooong hard days.
And this is how we re-pay:

We forgot
our
Mother tongue.

We forgot
Africa,
from which 'WE' come.

We forgot
how to just
hold on, be strong,
an'
run on.

We forgot
'ONLY' to speak,
when spoken to,
be still, pray first,
and then move.

We forgot
to carry our own weight.
We forgot
how to appreciate,
love,
and ignore envy
coupled with hate.

We forgot
on the Lord,
to 'JUST' wait!!!

We forgot
we rode on the bones

of them dear slaves.
WE SHOULD BE SO ASHAMED...

Don't even know our surnames?

Dedicated to: *Who are we anymore; who have we become? We forgot.*

A RocDeeRay Production

Love Category:

A Mother's Love Returned

By: Author Renee' Drummond-Brown

Her brain cogitated me
Her eyes saw me
Her ears heard me
Her mouth spoke for me
Her smile secured me
Her lips kissed me
Her nose smelled me
Her cheeks warmed me
Her shoulders carried me
Her arms hugged me
Her hands prayed for me
Her fingers fixed me
Her breast fed me
Her legs held me
Her back braced me
Her heart beat for me

Her food nurtured me
Her love loved me
Her soul ached for me
Her blood ran through me.
Her God protects me.
Her old age privileged her a receipt...
The debt WAS paid in full...
by none other than me.
Mother's Day was hard without her and me.

Dedicated to: *I Returned Momma to sender and paid her forward.*

A B.A.D. Poem

Drowned in One's Own Blood

By: Author Renee' Drummond-Brown

Familia from the Latin
of human society
is a domestic group in
birthed relationships. Recognized as implied by consanguinity.
Like-mindedness of opposites attracting plasma, gore and kinships
that compare and contrast by common threads and biological alignments;
transparent genealogy textured in (SO-CALLED) love.
So. Why then, does familia
drown ONE in their OWN blood?

Dedicated to: *Can you donate me yOUR life's-blood? Then be quiet!*

A RocDeeRay Production

Little 'girlz

By: Author Renee' Drummond-Brown

I'm a lil' girl
'playin house for free;
'inna a great big world
'wit enormous mistakes.
An' sir-named babies galore.

Some see a child.
Society deems' a whore;
relying on a system
to take care of me.
What they fail to see
my momma's
inside of me.

She too
'wuz this 'lil girl
'playin house for free;
'inna a great big world
'wit enormous mistakes.
An' un-claimed babies galore.
Some saw-her as a child.
Society deemed a slut,
relying on a system
to take care of us.

What they failed to see
my mom's in her mom
and the cycle repeats
on
an
on
an

119

on
an
on
OUR welfare comes,
faithfully
the third of each month...

Dedicated to:
Round and round we go. Where we stop? I don't know.
But...the names have been changed to PROTECT the guilty.
This for sure AIN't me, I do know.

A RocDeeRay Production

Peace Be Still

By: Author Renee' Drummond-Brown

"Be still, and know that I am God:
I will be exalted among the heathen,
I will be exalted in the earth"
Psalm 46:10 (KJV).
Peter even saw Him
exalted in the waters
and heard He raised Lazarus,
from tomb filled dirt.

Like Peter,
I've seen 'Your' miracles Lord,
which can only be witnessed
'if'
on one accord.

So, why then
does my faith deceive me?
Causing me to drown within my own
sea of misery.

Lord,
I've tread 'Your' waters to stay afloat
and even refused 'Your' bait before long.
'Your' Script (ure) kept reminding me
of the sun going down
and the late hour
turning into dawn.

The false Prophets storms
turned into tornadoes;
whirling my ship across the seas.
Just like

"Jesus wept"
all I could pray
was
"Master Please!"

The currents tossed me
to and fro.
'Twas anybody's guess
which way I land and go???

My raggedy boat
began
showing her holes.
Still yet,
I refuse to walk on water
to the Man who fed 5000,
with 2 fish and 5 loaves.

Even the (god's) boisterous winds
cried out for me to come;
"join in."
Without hesitation
I bailed ship
again, and again, and again.
Stretching my arms out to that foreign wind
and those waves on one accord;
while sinking fast with them,
in a sea of sin...
"My Lord, My Lord!"

Without faith
I begin to drown very fast,
but,
in spite of,
nobody, but 'You' Lord,

built me an eternal bridge
over troubled waters;
made to last!

Stepping out on faith,
I just had to trust
and walk those raging waters,
passing Hell's gate.
'You' skillfully caught me;
hook, line and sinker,
using
The 'TRINITY'
to create my fate!

On THAT bridge
I heard a singer sang,
"The winds and waves
shall obey thy will"and on the bridge,
I witnessed
'Your' Peace (simply) Be Still.

Dedicated to: *A Bridge over Troubled Waters*

A B.A.D. Poem

Stalker

By: Author Renee' Drummond-Brown

According to LEARNER'S dictionary; A Stalker's defined:
1: a person who closely follows and watches another person for a long period of time
in a way that is threatening, dangerous, etc.

2: a person who slowly and quietly hunts an animal (http://www.learnersdictionary.com/definition/stalker).

Well...He said, they'd be together
to the VERY end of ALL time.
Liar, liar his pants caught fire.
And he gave her reason(S) to track rhymes.

Tunnel visions born.
Hell has no fury.
Like a livid lady who's
lied to and scorned.

She stalks 'em
in her mirror
morn, noon, and night.
He's scared as hell; unaccustomed,
to this, 'kinda brutal fight.

Tunnel visions born.
Hell has no fury.
Like a livid lady who's
lied to and scorned.

He can't handle her truth.
Can't handle this 'kinda fight.
Should've thought this thang through
fore he got caught, like a thief
with his pants down in the night!

Tunnel visions born.
Hell has no fury.
Like a livid lady who's
lied to and scorned.

He told #2 and 3
the very same thang.
Now he's 'runnin round asking the Police
"what shall I do; this nut got me 'goin insane?"

Tunnel visions born.
Hell has no fury.
Like a livid lady who's
lied to and scorned.

3 girls pregnant at the very same time;
while they're ALL 'sleepin,
stalker's up 'thinkin
but he's steady 'claimin: "they ain't mine!"
Liar, liar pants caught on fire.
And he gave her them reason(S) to track rhymes.

Tunnel visions born.
Hell has no fury.
Like a livid lady who's
lied to and scorned.

Each day through her window
She WATCHES as he goes by;
AND THIS AIN't no temptations

'kinda Motown song.
'Somethins bout to go down!

Tunnel visions born.
Hell has no fury.
Like a livid lady who's
lied to and scorned.

He forgot,
he gave her a key to his house, car and heart
She allowed herself in...got her grind on...
and thrashed it ALL completely apart.

Tunnel visions DEAD.
Hell has no fury.
Like a livid lady who's
lied to and scorned in the HEAD.

He LEARNED on THAT day
He was "thee" stalker's prey.
sHE's the animal who hunts
quiet and slow. Now they both know
he birthed a prowler
who pursues his shadow wherever
their after-life roams to and fro.

Dedicated to: Liar, liar her heart caught on fire!

A RocDeeRay Production

Spiritual Category:

Give to the Poor

By: Author Renee' Drummond-Brown

When you give the poor;
give directly to them.
That way; you know, that you know, that you know,
they're at least, eating.
LEAVE THE MIDDLE MAN OUT!
For all he does
is steals' God's 10% plus...OUCH!

"He that hath pity upon the poor
lendeth unto the LORD;
and that which he hath given
will he pay him again"
Proverbs 19:17, my friend...
The King James Version.

Dedicated to: *"I'll work for food."*

A RocDeeRay Production

God, What Do You Want from Me?

By: Author Renee' Drummond-Brown

I try hard.
Bother nobody.
Why can't they see?
God, what do You want from me?

I try to love.
Advantage is taken.
Of me.
God, what do You want from me?

I give ALL I got to give.
An' then, I give some more (in deeds).
10% is ever-so-free.
God, what do You want from me?

I bow so low.
Faced to the ground.

Not a soul around.
Still far from perfection.
Precision knows not me.
But at least, I try.
I walk in humility.
God, what do You want from me?

I'm only human.
As human as can be.
But then again.
You 'oughta know. You created me.
GOD, WHAT DO YOU WANT FROM ME?

Dedicated to: *WHAT NOW???*

A B.A.D. Poem

Sisters Still Standing

By: Author Renee' Drummond-Brown

"Ye shall not need to fight in this battle:
set yourselves,
stand ye still,
and see the salvation of the Lord with you,
O Judah and Jerusalem:
fear not,
nor be dismayed;
to morrow go out against them:
for the Lord will be with you"
2 Chronicles 20:17 (KJV).

Lord,
we didn't come to the battle to lose,
Nor
was this cancer choice ours to choose,
So,
we brought 'our' ammo
which is
Faith, Hope and Love,
But...
the greatest of these is love;
So,
we remain steadfast to the faith
until we hear a word
from above.
Father...
'You' foretold us,
to set ourselves and quietly
"stand ye still,"
So,
we are not dismayed,
cause we know, that we know,

Your SALVATION IS REAL
and tomorrow is yet
another day.
You've been there with us
every step of the way.
Through the tears, fears
and
even up and down
those tiresome lonely hills!
Nevertheless...
we simply understand
Your 'PEACE BEING STILL'
Yes
we rebuke you
and call you out by name CANCER,
Yes
You've lost this battle,
cause we're in it to win it.
AND YES
we're shifting the blame,
by not speaking it
into existence.
Our Sisters Still Standing
will continue to Stand, Stay,
WATCH
and then begin to pray,
while the God of Abraham, Isaac and Jacob
fights for us
another day!

Dedicated to: My sisters Still Standing; keep on fighting the good fight!

A B.A.D. Poem

THE PERFECT RUNWAY MODEL

By: Author Renee' Drummond-Brown

He walked the bloody red carpet.
Carrying sin on His back. Received a sitting ovation;
while under sanctified massive attack!
"Crucify Him! Crucify Him!"
is what the mob yelled!
"Father forgive them please" was His silent prayer for them;
while conspicuously, on their way…"STRAIGHT" to monopoly's Hell!

Draped in all purple; no designer name.
Nonetheless, touting a crown of thrones-Euphorbia milii;
fashioned in vogue
from the spurge family.
Fitted. One of a kind.
Designed for a Jewish King.

Strike a pose! No! Never. Not He.
Selfies' was something,
He; Himself, The Trinity DID NOT BELIEVE.

This models faultless look
caught everyone's eye;
He took the runway by storm
with that distressed wood worn
as He hung silently
'onna chosen timber tree.
Crucified openly
for the ENTIRE world to see.
Strike a pose! No. Never. Not He!

Dedicated to: *Strike a pose! No. Not He! Lights camera…He "only" takes action!*

A B.A.D. Poem

The True Vine

By: Author Renee' Drummond-Brown

If God was the branch and I was the Vine
His branch(es) would remain Divine.

Could I conceive Divine Holiness?
Or would I be a mess?

Would I create man from the dust of the dung?
Could I show love to the least of everyone?
Would I gossip about that fallen man's dirt?
Would my Genesis allow that first family to hurt?

Could my Vine keep together Leviticus' laws?
Or, would I not forgive man's fall?

Would I bring forth numbers out of Egypt for all?
Would I allow Joshua to lose Jericho's battle?

Or...Would his walls crumble ever so?
I really don't know.

Would I ordain that great big Ark from Noah?
Could I promise a colored rainbow?

Would my Raven be fed The Bread of life or starve?
Would the dove have peace and know not love?

That's why I'm the branch and The "I AM" is the Vine my friend.
So, therefore, His ordained Words forever remain to the end.
"I AM the true vine, and my Father is the husbandman."
AND ONLY A TRUE VINE WILL GIVE UP HIS LIFE FOR A FRIEND!

Dedicated to: *Doubting Thomas???*

A B.A.D. Poem

Note* 5th Stanza, line 19 is a Biblical quote "John 15:1" King James Version.

THIS LAND IS RAVEN'S LAND

By: Author Renee' Drummond-Brown

That blackbird couldn't land,
to pluck from land;
olive leaf's off of the land
because she foresaw desert land,
inward lands,
"The Red Sea" in middle of the land,
the Black Holocaust land
intended for Indians land
cause history said this land
is your land
this land is my land
from the coast of California's land
to the New Stanton New York island.
No, 'twas not the doves land.
The Raven flew to and fro 'ov'r no-man's land
first.

Dedicated to:
"And he sent forth a raven,
which went forth to and fro,
until the waters
were dried up from off the earth"
Genesis 8:7 (KJV).

A B.A.D. Poem

Civil Rights Category:

"4 Little Girls"

By: Author Renee' Drummond-Brown

September 15, 1963;
should've been singing
4 'lil girls sittin inna tree
K-I-S-S-I-N-G!

Instead the worlds' left p.r.a.y.i.n.g
throughout our midnights'.
"Thank you Lawd, sparing Carolyn McKinstry's life!"
But why...the B.O.M.B.I.N.G?

Cowardly caller, giving McKinstry
minutes of three,
just in time for an Angels' plea
to protect all 4 from the debris.

God's Roll Call: Adie, Cynthia, Carole and Denise,
come home now, you've paid the price
and are, officially released.
Sound off: Adie, Cynthia, Carole and Denise.

A Saint once sung this song:
"When we all get to heaven, O' what a happy day it'll be"
Adie, Cynthia, Carole and Denise,
this song ain't for your murderers to hum along.

You girls carried God's House on your back
and "JUST" like Him, never said a mumbling word, under attack;
blown to the ground, rocks in your head, nails in both hands!
This is fact. Simply because, God made you black!

K.K.K., Remind you of HIM?
"So God created man in his own image, in the image of God created he him;

138

Male and female created he them"
Genesis 1:27, King James Version.

God's Roll Call Robert "Dynamite Bob" Chambliss, and you others,
not good K.K.K. to take your "Dynamite" where you've gone blood brothers!
Oh, you murderers WILL pay God's price,
for this unforgiving sin; you'll all die twice!

Thanks' Joan Baez for "Birmingham Sunday"
It's the lyrics in your song; we're able to face Mondays'.
16th St. Baptist Church & Dr. McKinstry, we thank God you survived;
to tell our story of "The Movement" and keep hope alive!

Dedicated to:
LEST WE FORGET those "4 BRAVE little girls" residing with their Father.
16th St. Baptist Church, Dr. Carolyn McKinstry and Artist Joan Baez.

A B.A.D. RocDeeRay Production

BLOODY SUNDAY!

By: Author Renee Drummond-Brown

Birmingham Sunday bleeds 4 girls....
Joan Baez rhythms Monday blues.
Addie Mae Collins' Tuesday's news
cries across the world with outpours.
Wednesday's weary blood, sweat and tears
Denise McNair's numbered as two.
Cynthia Wesley thrice echo's
over the hump. Thursday prides fear.

Carol Robertson =4
Minus Friday's unlawful plights.
Saturday night boast girls no more.
Freedom ain't free we gotta fight!
Sunday's blood has come and begone
If last is first...Sunday's still hard.

Father forgive them "please."
For they knew not "Sunday's BestIES"
innocent blood shed
that they IN FACT unlawfully poured.
Only justice can even their score!

Dedicated to: *4 lil' girls*

A B.A.D. Poem

BLOODY SUNDAY
MARCHES ON TUESDAY!

By: Author Renee Drummond-Brown

A last-minute call ....
Warranted a sound off,
of MLK marchin his funeral procession along;
past the Edmund Pettus Bridge, by the wayside of
blue blooded batons.
Judge, juror and executors rule to punish
peaceful protestors; walkin while black, sangin 'dem songs.

Turn around Tuesday was Martin's way
to text, tweet and show the world selfies
from Thy Kingdom Come to the least of ev'ryone.
Cause of 4 lil' girls, a judge sympathetically
was on the verge of granting a court order for peacefully
protestors not to be interfered by bluebloods'.

A mile and a half out of town
protestors walked that bridge up and down.
Helmeted troopers, horses, shotguns, batons, cuffs
and yes, hate rules on...
Lights camera action...CUT!
A prayer of reconciliation was said
and the people went home betrayed.

Dedicated to: *the late Dr. Docherty of the New York Abner Presbyterian Church.*

A B.A.D. Poem

Foot note* MLK-Martin Luther King Jr.

Emmett Louis Till; Sleep My Child and Finally Get Some Rest

By: Author Renee' Drummond-Brown

~You're gone
but not forgotten, so
sleep my child and rest.
Your mother who now joins your ranks,
always believed your mission was God's test.
...And now, I know my son;
LIKE HIS SON,
He only calls home His very best. So
sleep Bobo
with your FATHER and mother at your side and
comfortably get you some rest.

~The murderers that erred and stole you are now
the ones who rotten within their own graves.
As you have ascended into the heavens; the roles have now switched,
at this time Milam and the Bryant's
are on 'trial, judged and have-become
God's unworthy slaves!

~I too lost my Father's Son,
as well as you, my son, even before
I was born. But on this very day
I remembered you both...and I'll
forever mourn.

~EMMETT LOUIS TILL, you did not die in
vain. So go to sleep with your family
and be content.
After all, you gave us

"The Civil Rights Movement"
...and our very first
black President. Therefore,
because of you, Barack Obama, was heavenly sent!

Dedicated to: *The Memory of Emmett Louis Till.*

A B.A.D. Poem

Eyes off the Prize?

By: Author Renee' Drummond-Brown

What would our slain,
Jesus the Christ, John F. Kennedy, Malcolm-X,
and Dr. King say today?
If alive, would they say
"Somebody took their eyes off of the prize"
in a very sinister way?

Did we forget to remember 4 little girls, Emmett Till, Medgar Evers,
and Viola Gregg Liuzzo?
I remembered them through poetry as they are one of many
unsung fallen heroes!

I'll sing a song in the key of 'C' and write it down too;
reminding them you're not far,
your children's children live out your dreams and we don't even know
who they are!

Have we forgotten
The Father, Son, and Holy Ghost?
Have we forgotten
they shouldn't be the last resource used only
when needed the most!

Have we forgotten
The Scriptures through our hearts memorization?
Have we forgotten
when to speak, and when to be a quiet storm
through meditation?

Have we also forgotten
all of 'our' slaves?
Have we forgotten

that they too died so that
we could live to see better days?
Have we forgotten
how to talk to God, tithe, worship, fellowship
and pray?
Have we forgotten how to stand, stay, 'dream',
hope and obey?

Have we forgotten
the Church, our Bible
and
the one and only true Father?
Have we forgotten while on others thou are calling;
or
why even bother?

Have we forgotten
the Freedom Singers, Boycotts, Marches,
and
those Freedom Rides?
Have we forgotten
how to cry for freedom
with all jokes aside?

Have we forgotten
how to sing praises, dance and wade
in the water?
Have we forgotten how to sacrifice, make do, struggle,
eat leftovers, and even barter?

Have we forgotten
our elderly, children and family
or
is that root severed from the TRUE VINE,
Have we forgotten
how to be still, and wait on Him

to move in His time!

Have we forgotten Communication, Discrimination,
and
Segregation?
Have we also forgotten
our Salvation, Retaliation, Deprivation,
and the importance
of Education?

Have we forgotten
to keep our Eyes on the Prize?
Or
were our Eyes off the Prize
'cause' it's already won by those
who suffered, bled and died!
Have we forgotten
that we're not legally blind!

Have we forgotten
that famous
"I Have a Dream" Speech?
Have the entire 'Dreamer's' died off,
and the rest of us just
fell asleep?

Dedicated to: *The 'ONE' who remembers to never forget To Have a 'DREAM'*

A B.A.D. Poem

Fit For a 'King'

By: Author Renee' Drummond-Brown

January 15, 1929, legally born
Michael King Jr., was he.
Oh, you don't know? I'm talking 'bout THAT dreamer,
with the enormous~~~monstrous dreams!

Daddy King
changed his sons' name
after the great Reformer; Martin Luther, you see.
PERFECT...
because Martin Luther was ordained
to be-THEE Civil Rights Movement King!

Graduate of Booker T. Washington,
Morehouse, and Crozer Theological Seminary;
February 25, 1948, @only 19,
ordained into the Baptist Ministry.
Marries Coretta Scott,
and settles in the city of Montgomery
(Alabama to be exact).
And from Boston University,
received his Doctorate of Philosophy
in Systematic Theology!

King,
now joins, the bus boycott, after Rosa Parks,
just sits down; which was, a fascinating thing!
U.S. Supreme Court steps in
rules bus segregation
illegal. Now that's,
fit for a King!

Harlem
nearly killed our King,
when Izola Curry, did the unthinkable
'letter opener thing'.
But King,
felt no ill will towards her,
just wanted her to get the help;
she so needed!

Lunch counter sit-ins were a part
of that movement
and King would just not flee.
The reality
was jail without bail;
while Robert and John Kennedy
called for Kings' release.
King knew, non-violence, freedom
and justice was God's only reconcilement for peace.

Freedom Riders and Freedom Singers
were doing the dog on thing
for our Nation.
Once again (U.S) Supreme Court steps in;
outlawing segregation
within interstate transportation.
And with God for us
who could be against us;
was King's Prophetic and Special Revelation!

Commissioner Eugene "Bull" Connor
confirmed,
King and Abernathy were jailed.
This launched that Birmingham campaign
where King writes that famous letter from his cell.
Lest we forget; simultaneously the great
Malcolm X, also had his own autobiography to tell!

King marched on to freedom,
with 125,000 in Detroit and over 250,000 more in D.C.,
"I Have a Dream"
was the speech of the day, which still rings out
into the 21st Century!

The price of freedom
comes at a cost
that even President Kennedy was willing to pay;
while King experiences, hurtful rejections
and stoned by his own
in the very same way!

Because of King
the 1964 Civil Rights Act was passed into law,
which was an exceptional thing.
So, the awarding of the Nobel Peace Prize winner
was 'just-fitting for this type of King!

The voting laws were passed.
Marcher's marched on
and King went to the Mountaintop.
Memphis Tennessee
'onna ordained balcony
Reformer, Martin Luther King Jr., was fatally shot!
.......And 'all' was at a lost!
...But, we march an' sang on...

Not bad for a 16th Century Reformer's dreams
to be reincarnated again.
"We Shall Over Come Someday"
is still necessary
for 'dreamers' to dream and singers to sing.
Until someone else comes along
who is Fit For a 'King, to reincarnate this Kings' dream.

***Dedicated to:** Geneva College;*
Dr. Todd Allen and Dr. John Stanko
Thank you for feeding my soul:
Rhetoric of The Civil Rights Movement and African American Literature

A B.A.D. Poem

MS. RUTHA MAE HARRIS

By: Author Renee' B. Drummond-Brown

Thank you concerning the Movement,
with your gift of songs.
Thank you for knowing and singing
"It Was the Blood" *for me,*
while being done wrong!
*Thank you for singing about that **"Old Time Religion"***
that we so longed!

Thank you for singing
"Before I'll Be A Slave I'll Be Buried In My Grave."
Thank you for singing
"Just A Little Walk With Thee"
while being brave.
Thank you for singing
"He's got the Whole World in His Hands"
while Non Violence
was Dr. King's message of the day!

Thank you for singing our way in,
and out of those jails.
Thank you for singing
"I've got Jesus and that's enough"
with no bail.
Thank you for singing:
"He's so Real" *in times,*
when you were frail.
Thank you for singing
"We've Come This Far by Faith"
can't turn around,
and we won't go to Hell!

Thank you for singing

"Pass me not, O' Gentle Savior"
and hear my humble cry.
Thank you for singing
"Somebody Prayed for me"
and told Satan GOOD-BYE!
Thank you for singing,
"I won't Complain"
which made our oppressors wonder why?
Thank you for singing
"Walk in the Light"
while always being prepared to die!

Thank you for singing
"Precious Lord Take my Hand"
while you took that stance.
Thank you for singing
"How I Got Over"
while taking that chance.
Thank you for singing to kids
"I've Been In A Storm"
*and **"Respect Yourself"** in advance.*

Thank you for singing
***"I've Got A Testimony"** to President Barack Obama;*
*as you **'RUTHA MAE HARRIS',***
do your Holy Ghost dance
(In Song)!

Dedicated to:
Ms. Rutha Mae Harris, The Original Freedom Singer of The Civil Rights Movement and the
Black, Brown, Red, Yellow, and White men who bled and died for the cause.
THANK YOU ALL FOR YOUR INVOLVEMENT IN THE CIVIL RIGHTS MOVEMENT.

A B.A.D. Poem

Rutha's Freedom Still Dreams!

By: Author Renee' Drummond-Brown

"If the Son therefore shall make you free,
ye shall be free indeed" **John 8:36 (KJV).**
Rutha, those songs motivated the marchers
to march on with a King,
but, we shall overcome someday STILL
needs to be sung. Or
has we shall overcome; come and be-gone?
Just sing Freedom Singer,
Just sang on for all wrongs!

...So 'SANG' on
Ms. Rutha Mae,
as if, it's, the last song.
...Dance.

Like David danced,
with all your might.
Your chorus
rings out, for those of us
who are frighten.
Your melody is in tune
with none other than
the Triune.
Your Godly chant stops Satan's
unwanted blues.
Your hymns teach us
of the Father's Good
Infallible News.
Your track record is impeccable
with ballads to choose.
And with God before your solo-
we simply can-not lose.

...So 'SANG' on
Ms. Rutha Mae
as if, it's, the last song
...and then
dance the dance of David, while 'YOU' long
for 'our' dreams of freedom,
within those songs!

Rutha,
You smelled freedom in the 60's,
You tasted it in the 70's,
You touched it in the 80's,
You saw it in the 90's
You 'sang' about it in the 2000's
and 'I hear' in 2019, just like David's Psalms;
Rutha's freedom still dreams on...

I love you Ms. Rutha Mae Harris.
FOREVER 'YOUR' Pittsburgh Author:
Renee' B. Drummond-Brown

Dedicated to:
Original Freedom Singer of the Civil Rights Movement, Songbird/Activist,
Ms. Rutha Mae Harris

THANK YOU FOR YOUR CONTINUED SERVICE TO THIS COUNTRY!

A B.A.D. Poem

Tide Can't Get These Stains Out!

By: Author Renee' Drummond-Brown

Liberty and Justice
for all.
Plagues, distressing them black lives.
Do they matter though?
Causing their children's; children
all manner of post traumatic slave syndrome's plight;
equivalent to undaunted heartaches
and 'sho'nuff, grief, misery
an' some strife.
Does it 'REALLY' matter
though?

Who could've known
America would've grown
so very bold;
to reaping what She's sown?

Malcolm X knew;
their chickens would eventually
come home an' roost;
that's who knew.

True 'dat;
this is so, very true.
America, Tide Can't Get These Stains Out!

Dedicated to: *America; America, Father PLEASE shed some grace on thee.*

A B.A.D. Poem

Whistle Blowers

By: Author Renee' Drummond-Brown

A colored weighted body
seen by boys 'fishin, August 31, 1955;
gutted an' reeled out the Tallahatchie
River. The death angel cried! Wanted dead, not alive,
on August 28, 1955, in Money Mississippi.
The death angel cried!
An open casket
for the world to take notice and see.
The death angel cried!
From his death 'unTILL her death;
Momma, paused at her cherubim's casket
in total disbelief and sorrowful regret.
And yet, she knew the system was operating
systematically at the best of its very best.
52 years passed
before historical markers were erect
at a site linking to that boy's death.
That markers' shot up daily by friends
of the whistle blowers ACT, who, finally confessed,
that nothing that boy did
could ever justify her mess.

Dedicated to: The Whistle Blowers ACT...Take II. Cut.

A RocDeeRay Production

'X' Marks the Spot!

By: Author Renee' Drummond-Brown

On May 19, 1925,
born Malcolm Little was he.
Little did we know he'd die
a Minister in a Temple
for the entire world to see.

He attended Pleasant Grove Elementary,
West Junior, and Mason High Schools.
Although, didn't graduate top of his class,
make no mistake about it, this genius was no fool.

In life all he knew was hardship after hardship
and blow by blow.
His father gets ran over by a street car and dies,
or so were told
???

Little's mother Louise,
is committed to Kalamazoo
State Mental Hospital.
With nowhere to go, and everywhere to roam,
Malcolm's only option was
the juvenile home.

He confided his goal in a teacher,
to one day become
this lawyer figure.
Like Dr. King's dreams being ripped away,
the teacher replies not realistic for a "Nigger!"

Little was shifted in various foster homes
that were far from being heavenly sent!

159

Free at last, he moves to Boston
with half-sister, Ella Collins,
who is both strong
and independent!

Minister Little acquires job after job
and becomes a jack of all trades.
Shoe shining, dishwashing, soda jerking,
and on the railroad New Haven's boy slave.
These types of jobs he was master to none,
'cause he was ordained with a Minister X's reign!

Minister Little is exposed into a world
of hardened crimes. Specifically,
in Harlem (N.Y.),even the U.S. Army
found him unsuitable with various
mental and instability problems!

He goes by Minister,
Malcolm, Little, or
AKA in the streets (if you will) "Detroit Red."
Existing in a harden criminal's life of jail-cells;
while making for himself a hard bed!

Elijah Muhammad impressed Malcolm
with letters sent to his cell,
via U.S. mail. Minister Little converts, and receives the legendary X,
from The Nation of Islam, while still in jail.

Minister X, exchanged his I do's
with nurse Betty Sanders, to make his life more complete.
But for the life of X, he simply can't understand Dr. King's position of
"I have a Dream."
Until, his metamorphosis occurs in Makkah,
which color-blinds Minister X's dreams, just like Dr. King.

Because of change, like Dr. King,
and so many others,
X knew he had a shortened life span.
Being the genius that he was; in collaboration
with Alex Haley, his autobiography was well planned.

Malcolm X begins to 'SEE' beauty in humanity
while embracing the true Islam.
'X' marks the spot
in a New York City Temple
where he was fatally shot.
Lest his 'own' forgot what they too were once taught
by this great man!

Malcolm X
gave the Civil Rights Movement
"by any means necessary"
a much needed boost.
Like Christ, 'we've' judged him unfairly;
therefore,
"All of 'our' chickens have NOW come home to roost!"

Dedicated to: *Minister X.*

A B.A.D. Poem

Slavery Category:

25 Lashes

By: Author Renee' Drummond-Brown

25 lashes
for being
born black.

25 lashes
on that
auction block; stacked.

25 lashes
for bald-hair,
being too napped.

25 lashes
for another
house-slaves crap.

25 lashes
for Missy's
'lyin rap.

25 lashes
for Mr's., rapes
and repeated attacks!

25 lashes for
re-cleaning
this an' that.

25 lashes
for President Barack.
While Obama,
stayed under scrutiny;

we've grown numb
an' accustomed to
400+ years of massive attacks.

Dedicated to: *Oppression + slavery = sin.*

A B.A.D. Poem

America was Raised on 'MY' Breast

By: Author Renee Drummond-Brown

"Thy two breasts are like two young roes that are twins,
which feed among the lilies"
Song of Solomon 4:5 (KJV).
I raised America on my breast
and she never asked me
nor said please.

ALL of her children
gave suckling to my milk
morning, noon and eve.
But, she neither, either, thanked me,
nor said please.

My own children rode my back.
Simultaneously, the life was being sucked

from my breast while under
massive attack.

But. I 'sang' on.
"Oh' my soul 'gonna pick a bale of cotton"
until God
'done' turn that sun black.

But the Son
will
come out tomorrow,
an' lighten
the breast load of sorrows.

So, I may begin
to feed again,
and give suckling
to those who
unlawfully borrow.

O' Home of the brave
and
land of the 'free;
my milk was not for the taking;
you took,
advantage of me.

I ache for my African man.
Who, like our children;
he too, shares my breast
throughout the lands.

But my soul still manages
to find love
the best that it can.

I still cry
for 'Freedom'
for
the African man.

The African man
couldn't sip
from fountains
back then.
But,
the Wet Nurse was equaled,
not separate
while feeding those children.

Got Milk?
Be for real America.
My dairy is nutritious
as it comes.
Filled with calcium,
proteins
and
sweet brown love.

These critical nutrients
are gifts from above.
YES! I GOT MILK!
My breast is compared
to innocent doves.

Redefined by me,
and refilled
with the Father's ingredients
of pure love.

I
fed 'The Nation'
since
the beginning of time
with no regrets.

AMERICA WAS RAISED
ON MY
SWEET
CHOCOLATE FILLED BREAST!

Dedicated to: *The Wet Nurse Slaves, for a job well done!*

A B.A.D. Poem

δοῦλος [Doulos]

By: Author Renee' Drummond-Brown

S *egregation*
L *ocked-up*
A *partheid*
V *engeance*
E *nslaved*
R *etaliation and*
Y *OU DON'T SEE IT?*

Dedicated to: *U.*

A RocDeeRay Production

Flesh of My Flesh!

By: Author Renee' Drummond-Brown

She calls OUT unto me, from the grave!
Renee', she said, tell them:
"Archeologist, finally, found my grave."
Tell them, that you are:
the daughter of Eve's runaway slaves!
Tell them THAT you are:
bone of "MY" bone, flesh of "MY" flesh; who art "MY" child;
that they,
decided to, enslave.
Tell them Renee', to:
swab your mouth and there to WITHOUT A SHADOW OF DOUBT;
they'll find "MY" DNA.

As Amazing Grace would so eloquently sang,
I was 'neva lost, but, to them, I was finally found. So say their sir-name.
Lucy in the sky with diamonds was the celebrated music being played!
So say their sir-name 'CEPT tell them Renee',
"Lucy" is not "my" African name."
Tell them.
Tell them.
Tell them.
Tell them.
Tell them.
Tell them.
Tell them **#AL 288-1,** tags
my remains.

Dedicated to: Australopithecus afarensis (Tanzania, Kenya and Ethiopia).

A RocDeeRay Production

He Beat Me

By: Author Renee' Drummond-Brown

Massa please!
Done; done all you ask!
I cooked;
red rice and beans.
I cleaned;
scrubbing 'doze hardwoods on bended hands and knees!
Polished silverware for ENGLISH crumpets and tea.
Breast-fed those babies;
while calling 'em Ms. Missy!
Ev'n listened to Mrs. Millies' warrant-less pleas.
Stayed quiet while he be raping me.
Got up, an' attended your 'chillins needs.
Picked cotton 'inna field of fleas.
Ev'n watched a 13 year ol' Negro 'swang from a tree;
'screamin "MASSA PLEASE!" (guess, un-lucky).
Pled the blood 'fo me.
Plead the sinners plea...
Wondered if a Savior or Underground Railroad gone 'eva come 'fo me?
All 'dats left to do
is get, the lashes that await me
and start all ov'r on 'morrows journey.
He Beat Me.

Dedicated to: *So, deserving of me and them slaves.*

A RocDeeRay Production

"him!"

By: Author Renee' Drummond-Brown

*I luved THAT boy like no other. He's da only thang that belongs
half to me an' half to Massa's genealogy. Not ev'n da rag on my head(S),
shoes on my feets, or the big house I keep; claims me.*

*Half of him belongs to me. Half of him to Massa's genealogy! Massa luuuved when makin
that slave. Cept, I laid there witout a say. But I wuz too shrewd to make claims
an' give "him!" a name. Mrs.
Missy pretend to be blank. Think her kids IZ da only one's wit claims. Truth be told
he fathered most that he bought N sold! What a sheer shame! I raised Missy's kids on my breast just the same
while tuckin my feelins away, deeeeep into
my bosom ev'ryday.*

*Missy insisted that boy be hanged.
That's why I never gave
THAT
bastard a name.*

Dedicated to: *Massa Jr.*

A B.A.D. Poem

Negro HAND Me Downs and BRASS feet JUST Like Mine

By: Author Renee' Drummond-Brown

Atlantic TRANS
sailed my negro HANDS
to the Indians' stolen, HAND me down lands.
There my HANDS sold! To the highest bidding man.

But, while on THAT ship;
my magic HANDS cared for the negro sick
and these HANDS served Massa's nightly needs of cons and tricks.
But. My negro HANDS, so missed, the African garden, of Mother lands sheer bliss.

Once sold! Massa surnamed me BROWN.
My enchanted HANDS wuz' the best of the best in that Negro slaved town!
My precious HANDS picked his cotton from "Son" up to sun down!
HANDS down...Truth be told, I picked more cotton than the Lawd' aloud!

Sangin' in them fields; my HANDS clapped my FEETS' stomped.
Rump shakin' and HANDS swaying wit' these big boned hips, they rocked;
just like deeze' kids today, my HANDS bopped, bopped boppity' bopped!
These HANDS charmed and motivated the cotton pickers to never give in, give out, nor stop.

After my long dayze' wuz' done;
I still had to go FEED Mrs. Missy's son.
Twas' my Negro HANDS and black breast that gave the red, white, and blue sum'
dark chocolate love;
HANDS up…Mrs. Missy was as (c)rude as could be. Jus for the sake of havin' her sum' fun.
But God! Said my HANDS still had to show His infallible SON.

Massa, treats me like his dog; but, trust these HANDS 'wit-his food.
HANDS down…How asinine is that and what an oblivious fool?
My HANDS plucked his string-beans and I used his kitchen tools.
Thank God, my hearts' not like his; cause these HANDS could've took him out, IF,
I really wanted too!

My negro HANDS cleaned his nasty house.
My negro HANDS cleaned his child and washed Mrs. Missy's blouse.
My negro heart and HANDS are the foundation of the lost.
My negro HANDS talked all the day long, but, shut my mouth like a blaspheming church-mouse.

My HANDS couldn't wait, fo' Sunday to come;
so, my HANDS could praise Him, on high…up above.
Whiles' the preacher-man dialogued, my Hands clap and my feets' run
These HANDS gave God "ALL" the glory, but, this heart of mine, stole 10% of His Son!

Father-God, I held onto the faith an' kept my HANDS on the plow.
Oh Lord, my HANDS held, onto, the here and now.
Their "hands" were always too short to box wit' God's.
Yeshua, jus' like You; my HANDS and FEET are lined wit' negro copper. WOW!

So, jus' like these kids today, I waved my HANDS high in the air;
and shook my HANDS, and nappy-braids like I just didn't care!

But, not-nair, one person, bett-say', my HANDS were ever bare;
because, since the beginning of time, my NEGRO HAND me downs,
and BRASS "FEAT" were ever present there!

So you SEE...
YOU BETTA' ASK THE SCRIPTURES BOUT MY NEGROID LIPS, NEGRO HANDS AND BRASS
COPPERED CRUSTY FEET!!!

Dedicated to:
The Father's hand me downs. THAT BE ME! You betta ask sumbody'...bout me?

A B.A.D. Poem

Ocean Blue, What color are you?

By: Author Renee' B. Drummond-Brown

I see your hidden 'Black Holocaust' under the deep blue sea.
That is definitely my ancestor's blood, who cries out for me.

The bottom of those murky waters is certainly the color Black-Negro.
While the top layered sea, disguises the color Blue-Indigo.

As I see the sea toss, turn, in 'rage' against the rocks; this sight is very familiar to me.
The children you left behind on dry land act just like thee, with nowhere to flee.

At least you made it out of that ship as you float onto freedom.
Traveling Atlantic, Pacific, Indian, and Arctic Oceans' with the ability to go and come.

While your children's children, are stuck in 'rage' on dry land, with nowhere to turn or run!
Hush, Hush Somebody is calling my name.

Shhhhhhh;
It must be those seashells whispering again

"Are you still a slave???"

Although it's been some years since you've been discarded, and tossed away at sea.
I must agree it's better to float 'FREE' than becoming property on land; just like me.

Hush, hush the Lord is calling my name.
To define these floating voyagers tangled in seaweed and pay homage to the unnamed.

Knowing this I boil with rage; but had to learn to overcome.
Still yet, all that's left on dry land is 'contagious' Post Traumatic Slave Syndrome (P.T.S.S.).

"And the Lord shall bring thee into Egypt again with ships,
by the way whereof I spake unto thee,
Thou shalt see it no more again:

and there ye shall be sold unto your enemies for bondmen and bondwomen,
and no man shall buy you" Deuteronomy 28:68 (KJV).

Ocean Blue, What color are you?
You appear to be a Black Holocaust, under the deep blue sea; Is this true?

Dedicated to:
The floating voyagers who didn't make the Journey, but 'sailed' to 'FREEDOM'

A B.A.D. Poem

Slave Gal; Miss Mary Mack Ain't got 'Nothin' On You!

By: Author Renee' Drummond-Brown

Miss slave gal
Brown, Brown, Brown
'wit' skin so
black, black, black
an' 50
lashes, lashes, lashes
covering her 'WHOLE'
back, back, back.

She asked her
Massa, Massa, Massa
to 'jus'
repent, repent, repent
before he
noosed her, noosed her, noosed her
but 'NO' not
him, him, him.

He hung her
high, high, high
she reached the
sky, sky, sky.
Cutting off 'ALL' oxygen, oxygen, oxygen
and her supply, supply, supply.

Slave gal hung-her
head, head, head
an' then
she died, died, died.
She couldn't come
back, back, back
an' the onlookers 'NEVA'
cried, cried, cried!

Dedicated to: *Someone call 911.*

A B.A.D. Poem

SLAVERY Recipe

By: Author Renee' Drummond-Brown

Colonel Sanders special recipe;
cotton pickhen good.
Chickhen soup, for the soul:

Getyah' younghen from West Afrika;
or fieldhen will do.
Put it inna mixin boat.
Use a dash O' Red-Sea-salt.
Whip it real good, inna black mixing bowl.
Remove the Begg-whites and beat it all night.
This can be a noosence, so knot
to give IT civilwrites.
Stir it crazy fo 400 mo yrs., and REMEMBER,
turn thy letters against thyself.

Bake at 1619.
When it begins to rise.
Poke holes; drain the grease.
DON'T FORGET, again,
pierce its side.

HANG round, fo it to kool.
Necks thang u know...
You're eaten
'fingerlickhen good Colonel Sanders alphabet soup.
Mm..Mm good...

Nutrition Facts:

- *No artificial flavors or coloreds*
- *Excellent source of vitamin C*
- *Only 5 calories per serving whites*
- *Keep in airtight containers and refrigerate cargo for even longer storage*
- *For canning add 1 tsp to each colored one*
- *Works great for dehydration and/or lynchin produce*
- *Use in ALL negro recipes...makes for an excellent SLAVE soup*

Dedicated to: *Arrest, Bondage, Captivity (A, B, C...σούπα)='s SLAVERY.*

A B.A.D. RocDeeRay Poem

Still Waters Run Deep

By: Author Renee' Drummond-Brown

Still waters
ran deep. Obscured from trio's trade;
Europe to Africa to American barters
would-be oceanic route of that blue-blooded cargo enslaved.
More like encoded Negro's baptized by Lots' wife
'inna saline resolution and bathed.

Them African diamonds;
orlov if you will
crowed the middle passage.
And were grade-A's fiscal bills.
Plagiarized from their homeland;
flunking their test. Crossed ov'r Atlantics' oceanic bed,
heavy-laden, and yes, them diamonds & pearls
found deep seas' rest.

Often mistaken to be black in 'colour.
Them sandstones reflect un-cut negroid tones
'ofva very dark past. STOLEN, BOUGHT and SOLD
to a bidder...Cept, them still waters

planted her stones 'inna basin 'runnin hot & cold;
of black disguised nigger-linked chains anchored
thick as thieves! No shows! Afro Americans'? NO! 'dems Negros'!
So I'm told. Gossip; now that's what I heard.
Bailed ship! So that no-man could get their hands on 'em!
Now-that, oceanic floor, must in fact...reap what she sows!

The mountainous ocean
shrouded in mystery, drama and death
caused them stones to ACT
a black fool an' SAT in deep sea trenches
not limited to aseismic ridges,
abyssal hills and seamounts and guyots
and jagged linears.
Who goes there?

The legendary diamonds
hide their-image
in-reflections of a glass bottom boat rhyming
and rapping without mirrored rhythm.

Nonetheless, salt-waters run deep
at best. More or less. With black diamonds
who looked back to cheat
on standardized test.

Dedicated to: *Black Orlov*

A RocDeeRay Production

Wade in the Water

By: Author Renee' Drummond-Brown

"Now when I had returned,
behold,
at the bank of the river were very many trees on the one side and on the other"
Ezekiel 47:7 (KJV).
My heart knows 'da trees 'OUT' to get at me;
so, my mind wades
in the water's mystery.

Currents are high.
River rats lurk.
Crocodiles are sly.
But gators are worst.
So, I wade asking 'dem trees no questions why?

Silence fills their air.
Snakes and spiders appear everywhere.
Fatigue, illness and disease.
Dehydration comes.
But 'dem trees aint gonna get at me.

In 'da-night
treacherous rapids come.
Mosquitoes and insects bite.
Wondering how Noah survived?
But dos' trees still in plain sight.

Inscrutability takes over.
Fog lives in the mist.
Secrecy minimizes the danger.
Abstraction of 'dem trees eliminates the risk.

I hear 'dem dogs.

I smells' 'da man.
I feels' the leaves.
I taste 'da salt.
In hindsight, all along 'dem trees
been watching me!

"At the bank of the river were very many trees on the one side and on the other,"
'Gotta stick to 'da plan.
Just hold onto the Father;
WATCH 'DEM TREES THOUGH
and simply
Wade in the Water.

Dedicated to: *Holding on! Endurance.*

A B.A.D. Poem

WHO LET THE 'DAWGZ' OUT?

By: Author Renee' Drummond-Brown

"WANTED DEAD." NOT ALIVE!!!

EXTRA! EXTRA! READ ALL ABOUT IT!
RUNAWAY SLAVE ON THE LOOSE
THERE'S NO DOUBT ABOUT IT.
NO WORRIES THOUGH. THE GOOD OL' BOYZ ARE SURELY
GONNA CATCH IT, WITH
HAY & ALLEN'S LIVE STOCK OF NEGRO DAWGZ, WHO'S
UNQUESTIONABLY..."GONNA"...CATCH 'EM ALL!

And them good ol' 'boyz said
"Get them dawgs 'ov'r here.
I can surely smell that Negro's fear."

And the slave said
"Lawd, if 'dayze catch me
on 'dis day; I 'jus 'wanna be dead!
Can't go back; won't go back. NO! Not 'EVER' again.
Enslaved. No. Not there!"

And them good ol' 'boyz said
"Well, would you look here, at his clothes; on the ground, face down
and our 'dawgz KNOW that Negro scent anywhere!"

And the slave said
"Lawd. Lawd. Lawd. I 'needs me 'sum waters'
to bathe my nappy heads'.
I 'needs to wade like no other
from
the Leviticus curse that YOU LAWD, sent me, my sons, brothers an'
haughty daughters."

And them good ol' 'boyz said
"The 'dawgz scent 'IZ 'gettin cold.
That Negro 'dun found him 'sum water
from 'sumwhere; so 'um told. No worries though, at $3.'d00llas
a head, 'we'ze 'gonna find 'em, catch 'em, skin 'em AND
kill 'em DEAD! If it takes US all night he's 'gotta surface somehow. 'Sumwhere!"

And the slave sang
"'Waade in the water. 'Waaade in the water 'chillins.
I'm the 'chile that
'MoZez 'brang 'outta Egypt land. 'Iz 'gotta wade 'jus a 'lil 'whiles longer."

And them good ol' 'boyz sang
"Eeny meeny miny moe catch a Negro
by its toe if 'dayze 'hollas, DON'T let 'em go
Eeny meeny miny moe. 'Cuz ain't no sunshine 'why's 'you'z gone;
the SNOW PATROLS got its hounds on ground.
'We'ze 'fennin to castrate an' send you heavenly bound. Ain't no
sunshine while 'you'z gone."

And the slave pressed on.
Anyhow. But,
did I mention,

he's only 10 yrs. ol'? A boy.
Far less, than a man existing life minus
experiencing the 'feelins of added joy at hand.

And them good ol' 'boyz said
"Well, would you 'lookie 'lookie what 'we'ze got here; a scared Negro, all
draped in anguish, an' 'sum childish fear. 'We'ze 'gonna kill 'em,
right now. Right here. Tried. Tested an' proven by our MOB, who
surely ain't scared."

And the slave 'BOY' said
"Lawd, 'imma cast ALL fears
'onna God heard, not seen. But 'sumhow, I KNOW that I know;
You do care. Father, forgive them 'PLEEEASE
for they know not what they do. 'Iz ready
to be a man now an' hang
from a tree. 'Ev'n 'fo You."

The Father knows
ALL oxygen was cut off
as he 'swang. 10 yrs. ol' but, considered a man.
Eyes bulging from his head, sweat pouring, from
his glands. Breath slipping fast. Numbness in both hands; mob 'yellin
"swing low, sweet chariot, 'no-ones 'fennin to carry you home."

Boy's minds' the last to leave
as he FORCED
to
~SWING~ and become a man from a poplar tree.

BUT~~~~
THAT'S NOT HOW THE STORY ENDS.
JUST

AS SURE AS I ROSE AGAIN.
I AIN'T FORGOT WHAT THEY DID.
Signed~~~~THE FATHER,
WITH THAT BOYS BLOODY TEARS.

Dedicated to:
'Y'our' BLACK LIFE MATTERED ENOUGH FOR ME TO PEN!

A B.A.D. Poem

Sympathy Category:

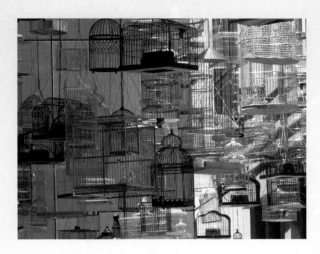

A Caged Bird Sings.

By: Author Renee' Drummond-Brown

Paul, I know why your caged bird sung. The
empathy she must've felt towards dat
Rizing Son.

On dem' slopes of no return, absolutely no glory.
*   No hope. She learnt da winds an' rains of a dark rooted past*
*   once closed her mouth but opened her doors.*

Free at las. Free at las.
*   Thank God almighty*
*   she too, iz free at last.*

A king of all queens
*   in the present future*
*   of a racist past.*

Witta latch an' steel key,
 locks could never meet. Dats why
Paul's bird would beat her wings.

But. Nothin but da' blood came ov'r she. Yeah,
 'his' bird
 could NEVA EVA sang.

His floated down stream like the calling of the Red Sea,
 drowning on her words as she so eloquently sings
 on the limb of a swing.

Chirping, Father, please, PLEEEASE, come see about me,
 as she peeps. Floating down stream holdin' onto bars
 his caged bird refrains; pleading, sympathy nevermore are we.

Dedicated to: *Sympathy sangs sad songs on 6-27-1872 and 4-4-1928.*

A B.A.D. Poem

Aged to Perfection

By: Author Renee' Drummond-Brown

Holding on is one of the hardest things to do.
As time tics your clock,
grey seeps in, hands wrinkle, eyes grow dim.
Wisdom comes (for some).
And the 'youngins think,
you're
a know it all!

Say cheese to selfies.
Caught on cameras are obsolete.
Nonetheless,
photographic memories
get lost, in the infamous, Alzheimer's disease...

Holding on is one of the hardest things to do.
As time tocs your clock,
balding seeps in, hands won't bend, and "I don't know them."

Wisdoms' lost (for some).
And the elders think,
you,
knew 'NOTHIN at all!

Dedicated to: *Archaic.*

A RocDeeRay Production

BIRD CAGE

By: Author Renee' Drummond-Brown

Even a jailed bird in search of a song
finds time to weep.
That Bird Cage will never allow him
to fully sleep.
The enclosed crate watches the clock
Tic, Toc.
Tic, Toc.

The coop he's in;
stalks from within
Tic, Toc.
Which is worst, the crate, or the clock
his mind's in? Or,
is it, The Caged Bird who sings;
cause none's there to talk?

Tic Toc.
all is at lost
Tic, Toc.

His freedom is unspoken words.
Prayers unreturned.
Cries that go unheard.
Feelings absurd.

Sympathy from this caged bird.

Alas
outrage!

No! Maybe it's the Bird Cage???
Cause Maya,
I don't know why a Caged-Bird would sing?

Dedicated to: *The late Paul Laurence Dunbar and Dr. Maya Angelou*

A B.A.D. Poem

Boy

By: Author Renee' Drummond-Brown

Oxygen
cut off
as he
swangs.
10 yrs. ol'
but
considered
a man.
Eyes bulging
from his head
sweat pouring
from his

glands.
Breath slipping fast.
Numbness
in both hands;
Mob yellin
"Swing low
sweet chariot
no-ones
fennin
to carry you home."

Boy's
minds'
the last to leave
as he
FORCED
to
swing
and become
a man
from
a
poplar tree.

Dedicated to: *Mr.*
LEST WE FORGET.

A B.A.D. Poem

Golgotha

By: Author Renee' Drummond-Brown

Went to
Golgotha today
in search of You.

Outside of Jerusalem's walls;
the good news said,
it was there,
You gave 'em Your all.

While there, I looked in the mirror
and saw
no reflection of You.
The images' 'lookin back
was sin and fear.

Immediately, I picked up a cross.
Picked out a tree.
And thought
Hmmh...I can't bear to carry the weight,
You carried for me.
Then I thought...
Stop thINKing too hard.
(You ain't there...You live in the heart).

Dedicated: *Calvary*

A RocDeeRay Production

Jaws (dun ta dun ta dun ta dun)

By: Author Renee' Drummond-Brown

18th & early 19th centuries---
changed its course of the great whites;
sailing Africa's coast off Atlantics' deep blue sea, swam;
blood 'suckin vamps who survived waterways off Negro's feed;
riding them waves for a chance, of love, at first bite;
of garlic-free, packed sardines, and
the glass bottom boat mirrored
Calvary's cross with Jews and jaws 'an
that's not all, Negro spirits dread at night;
their bodies sailing to Native lands feared:
slave trans!

Dedicated to: Canned sardines

A B.A.D. Poem

let it snow. let it snow. let it snow.

By: Author Renee' Drummond-Brown

tonight's snow, IZ
gonna blackout
them trees.
swing freemen
swing.

and the knights snow, IZ
gonna spread them sheets.
dream freemen
dream.

Dedicated to: *Since we have no place to go...let it snow.*

A B.A.D. Poem

Root Canal

By: Author Renee' Drummond-Brown

The mouth of the ocean
swallowed us whole.
She filled her pregnant belly
and claimed our souls.

Dark meat please;
the only meat she eats.
She prides fear;
while 'drowning-em in her tears.

That first trimester,
I solemnly do swear,
but, I know that you know
she swallowed our souls, WHOLE! PERIOD!
3 months more than anyone could bear.
Anyone else care
to cast a care?

The mouth of the ocean
swallowed us whole.
She filled her pregnant belly
and claimed our souls.

Dark meat please;
the only meat she eats.
She prides fear;
while 'drowning-em in her tears.

Trimester two;
subsided a bloody honeymoon. PERIOD!
But them slave babies craved oceanic-bed bottom blues.
13 to 27...very superstitious
(y'all) 'tween oceanic cargo crews.
'Twaz the very first time Mrs. 'Missea felt
that loathed dark meat move;
what a root-canal rush
to fill her gold-wisdom...ROTTED...sweet-tooth!

The mouth of the ocean
swallowed us whole.
She filled her pregnant belly
and claimed our souls.

Dark meat please;
the only meat she eats.

She prides fear;
while 'drowning-em in her tears.

Ain't hardly,
brushed her teeth in 'fo-hundred years!
Trimester prides 'negroid fears.
7 to 9 months,
laboring hard...
feeding from that salty-sardine cargo;
packed carefully
in impeccable canned-rows.
Dark meat; please?
Labor of lust
28 weeks.
Mind your manners. And your "own" business!

Black bodies floating.
Her pregnant mouth
is growing.
3 months of showing.
6 months of holding.
9 months of knowing.
The ocean-bed folds-em.
The ocean-bed holds-em.
'Cept
there nowhere to turn.
Nowhere run.
Dark meat please? Amen. Amen.
(I never learned to swim).

Black bodies floating.
Her pregnant mouth
is growing.

The mouth of the ocean
swallowed us whole.

She filled her belly
and claimed our cavity souls.

Dark meat please
is the "ONLY" feed
them TREES, OCEANS AND STREETS will feast!

Mind your manners... Remember, say your grace...
and please please pray
(Amen).

Dedicated to: *You 'gotta big mouth and you "NEVER" shut up!*

A RocDeeRay Production

Specks' of Dust

By: Author Renee' Drummond-Brown

Them trees have freckles;
'swayin the winds.
Every hole that dangles;
was a blackhead within.
Specks of dust. Spots as such.
Shared tween us
coloreds.

Freckles in the winds. Pimples of dust.
Hundreds an' hundreds
upon quintillions swung.
Them freckles in the wind are
merely-specks of loathed-dust.

Dedicated to: *Clearasil blemish and acne remover.*

A RocDeeRay Production

THE cart before the horse

By: Author Renee' Drummond-Brown

"Woe to the bloody city! it is all full of lies and
robbery; the prey departeth not; The noise of a whip, and
the noise of the rattling of the wheels, and
of the pransing horses, and
of the jumping chariots. The horseman lifteth up both the bright sword and
the glittering spear: and
there is a multitude of slain, and
a great number of carcases; and
there is none end of their corpses; they stumble upon their corpses"
Nahum 3:1-3 (KJV).
Never forget negro's them ol' carts prancing before the ol' horse and
bridling to draw up the head and
dropping down the chin and
disparaged in pure resentment about THE marching and
still IZ culturally expected, devine and
a jockstay prancing coffins through dem' filthy woods and
back dirt-roads in prehistoric times and
one can't beat a dead horse when they're already down and
yes they can; IZ' lied and
its sortta like an extinct animal being pranced upon and
sortta like a mammal lost in space-aged time and
a show horse gallivanting~~ 2 the tune of the processions and
fiddlers playin' on the roof and
juggling coffins like a circus clown and
might I may add; one of the best of the best noble acts in town and
mares on elm street and
charging stallions who can't compete with steeds and
no flags for him only them downy white sheets and
black nags marching alongside me crying after him and
equestrians gallivanting like an ugly black beauty whose deep inna sleep and
also laying in state as for waiting a prey, and
for a white sheet is a deep ditch; and

207

*THAT strange fruit is a narrow pit and
increaseth the transgressors amongst colored men and
colored women AND
do you know how many black bodies them trojans carted off in the woods?
I do AND*

Dedicated to: *Ashes to ashes; dust to dust; one of the greatest shows in town!*

A B.A.D. Poem

Trail of Tears

By: Author Renee' Drummond-Brown

Rain me a river inna trail of tears
and I'll show you displaced owners
forced to relocate their fears.

The 1820, 30, and 40's were not so kind;
for approx., 100,000 indigenous people
who walked miles while seeing blind.

Rain me a river inna trail of tears
and I'll show you displaced owners
forced to relocate their fears.

The Chickasaw, Choctaw, Creek, Seminole and Cherokee
migrated-tween Louisiana an' Florida, west of thee...
M.I. crooked letter crooked letter I.
Crooked letter crooked letter I. Humpback Humpback I.
river. Calling in, their reservations
while trailing sweltering tears behind.

Rain me a river inna trail of tears
and I'll show you displaced owners
forced to relocate their fears.

The $20 'dolla bill yalls',
responsible for the trails unreciprocated why's...
That love of currencies'
the root of all evil plights;
leaving its slurry residue behind,
with no logic, reason or rhythmical rhymes!

Rain me a river inna trail of tears
and I'll show you displaced owners
forced to relocate their fears.

The Removal Act guise
forced the home of the brave
red-men, round and about. But-why?

Junaluskas, who once saved the $20 'dolla-bills' life
inna horseshoe bends fight;
pleads for those Cherokee's rights.
But, the counterfeit currency, hid in his white-house like
a thief in the night.

Rain me a river inna trail of tears
and I'll show you displaced owners
forced to relocate their fears.

Dedicated to: *Evacuated landlords.*

A RocDeeRay Production

21st Century Category:

Bird's Eye View

By: Author Renee' Drummond-Brown

I saw 1000 blackbirds take mid-flight. Roaming
to N' fro. But.
Could not decipher which
were the ravens and which
the crows?

ONE
in particular stood out to me; cause He
was peculiar as peculiarity could be…And in His beak
was "THAT" pilfered olive leaf.

I thought…hmm,
alas
there You are! And wondered IF'
Noah knew; what ev'r happened
to You on that reigning night? Here You come again; in dreams
reincarnated into
Renee's Poems with Wings are forever Words in Flight!

Dedicated To: *Bye; Bye Blackbird. Take yOUR flight!*

A B.A.D. RocDeeRay Production

Can't We All Just Get Along? Hell Naw!

By: Author Renee' Drummond-Brown

Rodney King asked
"Can't we all just get along?"

I say...HELL
to the naw!
UNLESS. 'WE' 'WRITE'
'ALL' wrongs!

Raped,
hung,
burned,
beaten,
scorned,
shot
and yes,
'ev'n'
pic'NIG' torched;
while 'YOU'
spectators watched!

"Can't we 'all' just get along?"
Hell,
to the naw!
UNLESS,
you give 'ME'
'MY' 40 acres
'ANNA' mule.
And only then...
I'll be gone.

Other than that.
I say, HELL.
To the naw!

Dedicated to: *HELL, to the naw.*

A B.A.D. Poem

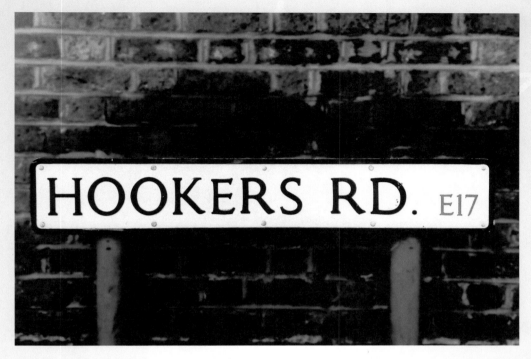

GARAGE SALE- (EVERYTHANG MUST GO)!!!

By: Author Renee' Drummond-Brown

He put his trash out in them streets
for any-an-everybody to take a sneak-peek.
The price was so so low.
It 'fo-sho 'gotta-go!
And without a-shadow-of anyone's-doubt;
WILL
definitely be sold!

The good, the BAD, and the ugly
WILL
shop till-they-drop;
thanking they's slick. Wanting 'SUMethin, for 'nothin, 'fo free.

John hits all the yard sales
(you see)
and the 911 prices, simply, can't be-beat!

EVERYTHANG MUST GO
before, the red, white, and blue
crowd, decides to show. Truth be told;
THEY, pick-up all the good deals FIRST,
before it-gets' a-chance...to be sold!

Toot-toot, hey,
beep-beep.
Clearance! ALL SALES FINAL.
They got 'dat deal of the week; real, real, REAL cheap!
Toot-toot, hey,
beep-beep..

Oh,
where's the sale?
Thought you never ask.
"SHE"
walks down
5th Ave.,
Madison,
Broadway,
and Times Square;
finishing her route on Wall Street, with-a pimps-pay
intact; like she just don't care.

Toot-toot, hey,
beep-beep...
GARAGE SALE 7 DAYS A WEEK.
24-7.
ON ANY OF THOSE CONNECTING STREETS;

216

The corner of Johns Way, and Hooker Street,
is where, her red-stilettos (heels)
meet and greet.

Toot-toot, hey,
beep-beep....

Dedicated to:
My hurting sisters (I'M BEGGING YOU) PLEASE come out them streets.
YOU ARE SO LOVED AND VALUED; more than you are weak.
Why should he get the sale and credit of the day, so very cheap;
while "YOUR" doing all the work standing on "YOUR" paved feet...
Sister's please...just think???

A RocDeeRay Production

IF, Innocent. Why Run?

By: Author Renee' Drummond-Brown

You asked...why do they run?
They're fleeing North
from them southerner's sons';
with ankle chains
and 'those heavy weighted shoes on.

But...IF, innocent.
Why then run?
They like not the caliber of Smith & Wesson's
company. Nor spewed imagery WHEN
FINALLY meeting their Blood.

Dedicated to: *Rock...take flight like a thief in the knight.*

A RocDeeRay Production

Let's Make America Great Again

By: Author Renee' Drummond-Brown

White bond servants, paid their way;
cross that arrogant-ocean, 'onna cruise ships
discounted rates (them coupon-clippers made-us, bargain of the day),
for Titanic vacationing slaves.
Who, (let me guess?) decided to stay.

Let's make America great again?
That door of no return
gave up Lady-Liberty's 'schlaged key
and not limited to her rusted ball and chain.
I threw that one in...'fo-free!

Let's make America great again?
The Dutch-ship; loaded with Afrikaans,
introduced them into the New World
of tobacco, cotton gin and farms;
who'd borrow, those crispy-cracked negro-hands
and feets...USED, to make America great again!
BUT.

219

WHAT ABOUT THE RED-MAN,
CLAIMING tHIS LAND,
AS his SO-CALLED LAND?

Let's make America great again?

Who we 'kiddin-
man?
The good ole' days ain't been so good and
the bad ole' days unquestionably outweigh the so-called good.
So.
Let's make America great again?

For who?
Cause "U.S." coloreds are still waiting
on Moses' 40 acres 'anna mules' foal too.

Dedicated to: *Liar, liar; souls required.*

A RocDeeRay Production

PLAN B in 'da house!

By: Author Renee' Drummond-Brown

Union measures, such as
Confiscation Acts and Emancipation Proclamation
in 1863, WAR; WHAT IS IT GOOD FOR? 'Everythang!
It ended slavery.
Removing those visible chains from one's neck, hands and copper-toned feet.

Party 'ov'r here! Party 'ov'r there!
While 'you'ze 'laughin and 'jokin...
The invisible PLAN B APPEARED!
The new improved slavery. Well let's JUST say;
for the sake of 'sayin...its 'SMOKIN!

AKA: DOPE!
Cloud 9

SUCCESSFULLY impairs one's judgement and 'mindS,
learning, freedom and memory. Addicting one, to loss realms of hope.
Forgetting to forget plan B effectively enslaves one, mentally.
Thus, hampering the user's ability
to think themselves as 'ev'r becoming free.

The dope certainly took us for broke.
Arresting the 'mindS
to plantation grinds as we so willingly smoke.

Now 400 years later...
We're back to Genesis.
Turning into our own traitors!
The new improved slavery has no color...
It's our mother's, father's, sisters and brothers
and perilous to say, Kanye, it's a choice, one to another.

Dedicated to: The 'ol effective back-up plan UNTIL we're back in visible chains AGAIN.

A RocDeeRay Production

Sequestered

By: Author Renee' Drummond-Brown

Who am I?
I don't know.
What am I?
I don't know.
Where am I?
I don't know.
When am I?
I don't know.
Why am I?
I don't know.

How does one not know?
Cause we're still in bondage; that's why!

***Dedicated to:** ALL RISE!*

A RocDeeRay Production

Sick and Tired of Y'our' Freedom?

By: Author Renee' Drummond-Brown

We have yet to overcome.
Unlike Fanny Lou Hamer,
You my precious children
are sick and tired of y'our' freedom???

Like the Father, its y'our' ninth hour,
Satan's here to see
who he can seek, kill and devour!

STOP singing "We Shall Overcome Someday",
Why 'NOT'
today???

Deep in y'our' hearts
we can't conceive;
that the Father instructed us
to simply believe!

Dedicated to: *'Our' 21ˢᵗ Century Children*

A RocDeeRay Production

Tainted

By: Author Renee' Drummond-Brown

Contaminated blue-blood
needs to be drained
from our hoods.
Without compensation;
waxed remains need to pile.
Their corpses must rotten and
spoil healthy. In exchange for rich-blood
using burial-oils.
Then and only then
once we have learned to boil;
we can plant seeds anew
onto eden's fertile soils.
And then rise like Angelou.

Dedicated to: *Still yet, we fall. We fall. We fell from grace. And they write us down in history.*

A RocDeeRay Production

Tar Baby

By: Author Renee' Drummond-Brown

15 holes deep.
1 tear. All covered in blood. Steep.
"Get on the ground! Face Down!"
Were the last instructions, he'd meet.

His cell phone rings.
The answering machine 'sangs.
"Wut up? I can't come to the phone right now.
My back conceded to:
Bang. Bang. Bang. Bang. Bang. Bang. Bang. Bang. Bang. Bang. Bang. Bang. Bang. Bang. Bang.
15 times and then 'sum. Plus, for the one's they lied-bout!
Please tell Momma, I love her;
(and his cell phone drops)...I'm out!"

Momma weeps; doubting Thomas' tweet.
"Cellphone. No gun! Should've; run spot run! They shot-em down

like a backward god;
in them Northern asphalted streets
showing blacktop, no 'kinda-mercy, respect nor luv.
15 spots deep covering that Downy white sheet.
Why'd he run?
Clorox. Bleach kills 99.9% germs, bacteria and
truth be told he saw their guns!
He heard the man
"Get down on your knees!"
And that's the legend of Tar Baby's pleas;
walking while black
on their City-owned paved streets."

Dedicated to:
Until the next-one bites the dust; later on this very day! And another one gone,
were used to it. But...for how long?

A RocDeeRay Production

The Central Park 5

By: Author Renee' Drummond-Brown

*WARNING! This poem contains
graphic descriptions of A severe violent crime.
Totaling 5
negro's and Latino's;
wanted DEAD! Not ALIVE!
Wrongfully convicted of raping that white gal;
jogging through life 'onna dime.*

April 19, 1989,
dragged through them weeds
that white-gal cried.
Clothes stripped from thee
that white-gal cried.
Bludgeoned, raped and sodomized
that white-gal cried.
Exposed to them trees that lynched Negro's 'fo free
that white-gal cried.

Thank God, that white gals' found, ALIVE
and not dead...her DNA cried!

But the wolf pack; prey of 5;
"innoCENT" presumed guilty,
WILL 'NEVA 'EVA
TOTALLY "BE" set FREE!

Lest we forget;
visiting family in Money, Mississippi
Emmett Till's
brutally murdered for "allegedly"
flirting with THAT white-gal you see.

Although, the Bryant's and Milam
confess their mess;
"ALL" are wanted "ALIVE" not dead!
Neva convicted of murdering THAT black boy;
who survived his shortened life-span 'onna dime.

August 28, 1955,
dragged through weeds
Emmett Till cried.
Made to carry 75 lbs., O' cotton-gin fan, to the river-bank of the Tallahatchie
Emmett Till cried.
Clothes stripped from thee

229

Emmett Till cried.
Exposed to them trees that lynched Negro's 'fo free
Emmett Till cried.
Bludgeoned, gouged out eyes, barbed-wired to a cotton-gin and shot in his head by thee;
Emmett Till died!
At least that that white-gal
lived to cry.

Momma Till prayed;
pausing at her son's mirrored casket 'fo the rest of her days,
Momma Till cried.
His horrific encounter refrains
Momma Till cried.
The guilty confess and "JUST" walk away
Momma Till cried.

Emmett Louis Till WILL 'NEVA-EVA BE
Momma Till cried.
Until her death came for thee.
Momma Till, was never EVER "set" free.

Dedicated to: *Don't you know Wolf's run-in packs?*

A RocDeeRay Production

230

The Choice is Up to You?

By: Author Renee' Drummond-Brown

"When you hear about slavery for 400 years…For 400 years? That sounds like a choice" (Kanye West).
"NO IT DON'T; IT SOUNDS LIKE SIN" (Renee Drummond-Brown).

The Home of the brave and land of the Free
allowed us to choose
designer irons used for our neck, minds', hands, and our feet;
anchor ring, ankle rack, belly chains, bending fiber, blindfolds and body chains.
Think I'll go with the anchor ring?
SWEET!

The Home of the brave and land of the Free
allowed us to choose which Atlantic Slave Trans we'd ride
when sailing the soft raging seas;
La Amistad' or Lord Ligonier (either-one, don't matter) would certainly be
suitable for my ancestors
and me!

The Home of the brave and land of the Free
allowed us to choose to leave WEST Africa, in 1619,
an' settle in Virginia's, extravagant
HGTV's plantation colonies.

The Home of the brave and land of the Free
allowed us to choose
those wonderful auction blocks to be sold away from
our natural families.

The Home of the brave and land of the Free
allowed us to choose
stunning surnames and become "made in the USA's" private property.
Brown, suits my family's name, just fine, (by me).

The Home of the brave and land of the Free
allowed us to choose
gods'
which stripped us away from our spirituality
and separate us from the true God of Israel
who, was meant to be.

The Home of the brave and land of the Free
allowed us to choose
losing our unusable mother tongue;
to speak, Ebonics, so eloquently.

The Home of the brave and land of the Free
allowed us to choose
being handsomely raped
EVER so "freely."

The Home of the brave and land of the Free
allowed us to choose
picking snuggly-cotton sun-up to sun-down;
wage-free.

The Home of the brave and land of the Free
allowed us to choose
straightening combs, jheri curls, weaves and perms;
I'll stick to Bo Derek's, invented braids, for sure. No; maybe, swag me
some, blondes have more fun, twisty's.

The Home of the brave and land of the Free
allowed us to choose
giving our sweet chocolate milk away
to ANY and EVERYBODY'S babies!
What a willing wet-nurse treat???

The Home of the brave and land of the Free
allowed us to choose
"our Studs"
to produce more babies
for fiscal slavery.

The Home of the brave and land of the Free
allowed us to choose
improper foods
for our privileged families.

The Home of the brave and land of the Free
allowed us to choose
no hats, coats, gloves or Cam-shoes
for our pampered spa-polished feet.

The Home of the brave and land of the Free
allowed us to choose
which whips, we prefer be-used,
WHILE being beat.

The Home of the brave and land of the Free
allowed us to choose
which garden of Eden trees
we wanted to swing!

The Home of the brave and land of the Free
by all means,
allowed us to choose
400 years of tormented pleas.

IF,
the Home of the brave and land of their Free
truly allowed us a choice
to be or not to be

233

enslaved...
Betta by golly wow; without, a shadow of a doubt,
we'd certainly choose 400 more years of delightful "evil-plagued" slavery
while giving it "our" finest praise and shout!
2 THUMBS UP!
SLAVERY "WAS NOT" A CHOICE Kanye,
without a shadow of a slaves doubt.

ACCORDING TO Google.com,
(https://www.google.comsearch?q=define+choice&oq=define+choice&aqs=
chrome..69i57j0l5.4261j1j7&sourceid=chrome&ie=UTF-8)

Choice

CHois

noun
1.
an act of selecting or making a decision when faced with two or more possibilities.
"the choice between good and evil»

synonyms:	option, alternative, possible course of action
	"you have no other choice"

Dedicated to:
Shake it to the east; shake it to the "WEST";
our choice will be slavery Kanye, which we truly love the best!

A RocDeeRay Production

What's A Stud to Do?

By: Author Renee' Drummond-Brown

What's a stud to do? "YOU"
taught 'em to be
free loading Freddie's,
shuffling their feet,

sailing/selling them to the Land of The Free to produce
more slave-men and wench-hened' breeds.
And now, "YOU" can't understand
why they don't get off the sheets;
'pullin up their own boot-straps man,
and onto their "LAZY" feet!...

What's a stud to do? "YOU"
taught 'em bout jail. Remember good 'ole Virginia, 1619;
them 2-chains up 'N 'runnin
on their necks, hands, mind and feet?
And now, "YOU" can't understand why they're still jobless in 2019.
Maybe their "RECORDS" hold the key?
I don't know. (Limited education). "YOU"
tell me?

What's a stud to do? "YOU"
taught 'em their profession was/IS a slave.
Labor for no pay.
And now, "YOU" can't understand why they sleep-in and leech
on "THE" system all day.

What's a stud to do? "YOU"
taught 'em not to feel a thang.
And now, for the life of "YOU,"
can't understand why they walk 'round
dejected, neglected and rejected;
showing no 'kinda love...like some hard-core thugs...
REMEMBER: crips and bloods;
touting "YOUR" dope, chains and guns
(they've no-ships, planes nor trains to 'brang "THAT" junk into the hood)!...

What's a stud to do? "YOU"
taught 'em how to be beat.

And can't understand why hurt people hurt innocent
people on "YOUR" clean, paved, magnificent
(blood on your hands) city stained streets...

What's a stud to do? "YOU"
taught 'em how to dress for less;
holes in their shoes, cut up shirts, trousers
too small, with undergarments shown...And now, can't understand
why they bust a sag "WHEN/IF" "YOU" decide
to let-em' in & out of-jail man...

What's a stud to do? "YOU"
taught 'em bout that-dope!
Remember those experimental drugs; helping them to cope?
Just Google medical experimentation on slaves
and you'll come up with a "boat-load" of links...fo sho!
LIKE...Cotton "CAME" to Harlem.
And don't act like, "YOU"
don't know?...

What's a stud to do? "YOU"
taught 'em to separate from family, friends and foe.
And now, can't understand why they drop their litter
from woman to woman...home to home,
no shows, and get ghost...as they, seductively roam, to 'N fro;
leaving behind an' Ark of blackened birds,
to fend, in "yOUR" madness all alone...

America "YOU" taught this man
in "YOUR" systematic scheme of things
how to master "YOUR" designed plan.
And now, they've perfected "YOUR" professional game;
to the best of their god given abilities and talents they bring.
And now, "YOU" no longer 'wanna play.
What a shame?...
Well, pat "YOURSELVES" on the back

237

cause "YOUR" studs have designer hardened-hearts.
And yes, they got it like that! 2 snaps!!
And whether "YOU" like it or not "YOU'RE" in this game!
Now that's what's up...

What's a stud to do?
I guess all these thangs "YOU" taught 'em 'IZ
some real FAKE NEWS too.
Stay tuned at 11:00!
And let "YOUR" news do what it do?

Dedicated to: *Fake News at 11:00 pm. Stay tuned!*

A RocDeeRay Production

You ain't 'gone believe this...
GUESS WHAT I HEARD?

By: Author Renee' Drummond-Brown

She told it to me.
I ONLY told it to you.
You ONLY told it to he.
He ONLY told it she.

And it was different;
time-it got back to you.

Be careful
who ALLLLLLLLLLLLL
you're telling it to...
Dedicated to: *Shhh...don't say 'nothin to ANYONE!*
Tell it to God. You won't hear it again.

A B.A.D. Poem

Indebtedness to:

MY BELOVED MOTHER The late BARBARA ANN DRUMMOND,
and my earthly father, Peter Charles Drummond, also my better-half, and our three children,
words cannot express the love that I feel for each of you,
so, I do what I do best and write the words on paper. Thank you family, for loving me unconditionally.

To my brothers Delbert Dwayne Drummond and The late Pastor Shawn Charles Drummond,
because of you, I learned how to become strong. I thank you both for teaching me life's lessons along this
journey-way. I Love you more than my words can express in this written form.

Others who have inspired my writings along the way,
mainly those American 'SLAVES' and because of them, I know how to survive.
I thank my ancestors for their unconditional service to this country!

Acknowledging, author Phillis Wheatley, for leaving a legacy as being one of the best prolific poets in pre-19th
century America and for showing the world that blacks are creative and intellectual. But, most importantly, I
thank God for using her to be the catalyst that bridged my poetry over our troubled waters into the 21st century.

Activist, Ms. Rutha Mae Harris, Original Freedom Singer of the Civil Rights Movement,
Thank you for 'SANGING' to me along my 'Straight and Narrow Path.'

Publisher Mrs. Judith Hampton-Thompson, Metro Gazette Publishing Company,
Thank you for 'Mending My Broken Wings.'

The late Dr. Maya Angelou, taught me how to rise within my writings and because of her;
"Still I write,
I write,
I'll write."

WRITING IS MY OXYGEN
~~~~~~~
"Renee's Poems with Wings are Words in Flight"
<<<<<>>>>>

240

Biography

Renee' Drummond-Brown is a renowned author from Pittsburgh, Pennsylvania. She is a graduate of Geneva College of Western Pennsylvania and The Center for Urban Biblical Ministry (CUBM). Renee' is still in pursuit of excellence towards her mark for higher education. She is an accomplished poetess with experience in creative writing and authored several books to her credit. Her work has recently been nominated by the Scarlet Leaf Review's list for "Best of the Net" nominations, 2018. September, 2018, Wildfire Publications Magazine awarded Renee's poem "BLACK CRIMES MATTER" Poem of the month. She has numerous works published globally which can be seen in cubm.org/news, KWEE Magazine (Liberian L. Review), Leaves of Ink Magazine, Raven Cage Poetry and Prose Ezine, Scarlet Leaf Publishing House, SickLit Magazine, The Metro Gazette Publishing Company, Inc., Tuck, and Whispers Magazine, amongst many others. Because her work is viewed on a global scale this solidifies her as a force to be reckoned with in the literary world of poetry. Renee' is inspired by non-other than Dr. Maya Angelou, because of her, Renee' posits "Still I write, I write, and I'll write!"

"God is our refuge and strength, a very present help in trouble.
Therefore will not we fear, though the earth be removed,
and though the mountains be carried into the midst of the sea;
Though the waters thereof roar and be troubled,
though the mountains shake with the swelling thereof
Selah" Psalm 46:1-3 King James Version (KJV).

We carry on.

Father. It is finished.

Printed in the United States
By Bookmasters